Hollywood On Ronald Reagan

Friends and Enemies Discuss Our President, The Actor

By the same author:

The Unkindest Cuts: The Scissors and the Cinema
Susan Hayward: The Divine Bitch
Down the Yellow Brick Road: The Making of The Wizard of Oz
The Golden Age of "B" Movies

HOLLYWOOD ON
RONALD REAGAN

Friends and Enemies Discuss Our President, The Actor

By
Doug McClelland

faber and faber

Library of Congress Cataloging in Publication Data

Library of Congress Cataloging in Publication Data
McClelland, Doug.
    Hollywood on Ronald Reagan.

    1. Reagan, Ronald.   2. Moving-picture actors and
actresses—United States—Biography.   3. Presidents—
United States—Biography.   I. Title.
PN2287.R25M38   1983   791.43′028′0924 [B]   82-25145
ISBN 0-571-12522-0 (pbk.)

Published by Faber and Faber, Inc.
39 Thompson Street
Winchester, MA 01890
Copyright 1983 by Doug McClelland

ISBN 0-571-12522-0
Library of Congress Card Number 82-25145
Printed in the United States of America

This book is dedicated to my ten-year-old neighbor
THOMAS JOSEPH NOWLAND

Program

Hollywood On Ronald Reagan

Friends and Enemies Discuss Our President, The Actor

The Cast

Gratitude is the memory of the heart.

J. B. **Massieu**

Starring in *Hollywood on Ronald Reagan* are exclusive interviews with, and comments from, Hollywood film personages who have known Ronald Reagan, or who simply wish to share their thoughts on the movie star who became President of the United States. Featured are quotes on President Reagan from the movie magazines and Hollywood trade papers during his almost thirty-year incumbency as a motion picture actor.

My deepest gratitude for their invaluable personal cooperation on this book to the following people:

DOROTHY ADAMS	JOAN FONTAINE
DAME JUDITH ANDERSON	COLEEN GRAY
ED ASNER	JOY HODGES
NOAH BEERY	ROBERT HORTON
BARBARA BILLINGSLEY	HOWARD KOCH
JANE BRYAN	JOAN LESLIE
MARGUERITE CHAPMAN	VIVECA LINDFORS
FRANK (JUNIOR) COGHLAN	STEPHEN LONGSTREET
NANCY COLEMAN	LEE PATRICK
BOB CUMMINGS	IRVING RAPPER
ROSEMARY DeCAMP	VINCENT SHERMAN
FRED de CORDOVA	PHYLLIS THAXTER
OLIVIA de HAVILLAND	DOROTHY TREE
PHILIP DUNNE	JAMES C. VAN TREES, JR.
GERALDINE FITZGERALD	GEORGE WARD
RHONDA FLEMING	MARIE WINDSOR

Then there are those players who had acted with Ronald Reagan and when queried recently for recollections or comments offered courteous but succinct regrets:

Virginia Christine (who appeared with Reagan in the film *The Killers*): "I just can't place him."

Margaret Hamilton (who appeared with Reagan in the film *Angels Wash Their Faces*): "My only vague memory of Mr. Reagan is when he was President of the Screen Actors Guild. But other than seeing him at one SAG meeting, I know nothing about him. Had I but known!"

Kim Hunter (who appeared with Reagan on television): "It was so long ago that any memories I have are too misty to be brought forth for publication. It wouldn't be fair to all three of us."

Mary Stuart (who appeared with Reagan in the film *The Girl from Jones Beach*): "I've wracked my brain, but I can't come up with any memory of our President."

To the many other individuals and publications quoted, sincerest thanks also; likewise, to the various publishers and TV programs — in all, a cast of dozens unfortunately too space-consuming to mention in toto on this page.

In addition, I am grateful to:

Academy of Motion Picture Arts and Sciences Library, Arthur Bell, The Bradley Beach Public Library, Eddie Brandt, Loraine Burdick, Paul Denis, Julie Cawthon, Charlie

Earle, Film Favorites, Charles Finley, Alex Gildzen, George Haddad-Garcia, Jerry Ohlinger's Movie Material Store, Jeanne Jones, Richard Lacey, The Library of Lincoln Center: The Theater Collection, Beverly Linet, Ted Macdonald, Jim Meyer, Eduardo Moreno, Movie Poster Service, Movie Star News, Vicki Pagliaro, James Robert Parish, Stephen Sally, Luke Starnes, Charles K. Stumpf, Jorge Tablada, Lou Valentino, Jan Wall, William Wolf and Rogers Worthington.

Special billing must go to Miss Geraldine Fitzgerald, who is as rewarding to know personally as she is practicing her myriad theatrical skills. Not only did this busy lady endure with characteristic grace several phone calls from me concerning this project, she also very kindly — and successfully — made long distance calls at her own expense to help me locate Hollywood people to be interviewed for this book.

Finally, I must thank my mother, who is always encouraging and helpful but found reason to be even more so with *Hollywood on Ronald Reagan*. We learned that Nancy Reagan's maternal grandmother was a Virginian named Sarah Whitlock who married a Charles Luckett and bore nine children. My mother, born Elna Whitlock in New Jersey, had a cousin, now long deceased, who was a leading educator in the state and also named Sarah Whitlock. Whether these Whitlocks are all actually "kin" is a question for the geneologists; but meanwhile Mom enjoys telling everyone she may be related to our First Lady.

Doug McClelland
Summer of '82

Close-Up

Biography is a region bounded on the north by history, on the south by fiction, on the east by obituary and on the west by tedium.

PHILLIP GUEDALLA

"My existence turned into one of those rare Huck Finn–Tom Sawyer idylls," our President has said of the young Mr. Reagan.

Born in a flat above a general store in the small Illinois town of Tampico on February 6, 1911, Ronald Wilson Reagan ("always pronounced Ray-gan") was the second son of Jack Edward and Nelle Wilson Reagan, whose first-born, Neil, was two years older and nicknamed "Moon." Just arrived and screaming, the future President of the United States was promptly rendered the sobriquet "Dutch" when his father observed, "For such a little bit of a Dutchman, he makes a hell of a lot of noise, doesn't he?" Actually, Reagan père was first generation Irish Catholic, witty, an ardent Democrat and ambitious, but fated by alcoholism to remain a shoe salesman.

"He had the Irish disease," Ronald Reagan later said of his father.

His daughter Patti has recalled, "I've heard my father talk about Christmases where the little money they had would go to alcohol. I guess anything like that you go through in your life makes you stronger, and I think that's made him stronger. I think he is forgiving of the situation. But it was hard for him to deal with."

If Jack Reagan was a pessimist, wife Nelle, Protestant and of Scotch–English descent, was an optimist. Ronald inherited more than his religion from Nelle. Despite her modest means (the family had lived only in rented dwellings until Ronald, having made it in Hollywood, bought them their first house there), she was well known for her charitable efforts. In addition, Nelle Reagan was, as her youngest put it, "the dean of dramatic recitals for the countryside. . . . Naturally I was pressed into protesting service—usually as the thing in a sheet at the Sunday school pageant with a character name such as 'The Spirit of Christmas Never Was.' It may be argued that my dramatic yen started at this point."

Bringing to mind Mark Twain's "infernal boys," Ronald, while growing up in early 20th century mid-Western America, was more attracted to treasure-filled attics, woodland mysteries, picnics, swimming in a treacherous canal, ice skating and the forbidden excitement of playing with a shotgun that blasted a hole in a friend's ceiling. There were his first long pants (hand-me-downs from his brother) . . . rigged watermelon hunts in college . . . a life-long love of horses.

And there was football, his favorite pastime of all.

For brief spells the family lived in Chicago, Galesburg and Monmouth, Illinois, then back to Tampico. When Ronald was nine they settled in Dixon, Illinois, about ninety miles from Chicago and somewhat larger than the municipality of his birth. The Rock River runs right through its middle. Dixon became the place Ronald Reagan called his home town. Working for seven summers as a lifeguard at Dixon's Lowell Park, he claims to have saved seventy-seven people from drowning. At fourteen and a recent arrival at North Dixon High, he also began saving to attend Illinois' small Eureka College, and did so finally in the fall of 1928, majoring in economics and sociology, minoring in dramatics. A sports scholarship covered half his tuition, but mostly he worked his way through washing dishes as well as lifeguarding.

In 1982, Eureka alumnus Neil Reagan said, "He wasn't first string (on the football team)—I was. I was a good student—he wasn't." Adding, "Ronald and I were never really enemies but we never really ran around together." A still married Neil Reagan said that he never quite forgave his brother for "stage-whispering" forty-six years earlier at Neil's one-and-only wedding, "I'll give you two to one it doesn't last a year."

The Reagans: John E. Reagan, Ronald's father; brother Neil; Ronald; and his mother, Nelle Wilson Reagan. Portrait was taken in Tampico, Illinois, circa 1913.

★ ★ ★

Acting in college plays convinced the young Ronald that some area of show business would be his goal.

Station WOC in Davenport, Iowa, hired recent college graduate Reagan as a $10-a-game, play-by-play sports announcer, which led to a more prestigious appointment in a similar capacity at WHO Radio in Des Moines, Iowa, and, subsequently, $75 a week. His duties at WHO included announcing the Chicago Cubs' baseball games. In 1937 the station gave him his own show, *Today's Winners*, and he embarked on his fateful California trip to report on the Cubs' spring training at Catalina Island.

When Reagan revealed his desire to be in films to his Hollywood actress friend Joy Hodges, she introduced the good-looking aspirant to her agent, George Ward of the William Meiklejohn Agency, who was able to arrange a $200-a-week contract for him at Warner Brothers Studios in almost record time. With equal dispatch, Warners gave the glib, extraverted novice the lead of, appropriately, a radio announcer in a "B" movie called *Love is on the Air*, and released it that fall.

While producing its share of fluff, Warners was known as the most socially conscious of the half-dozen or so major "golden age" Hollywood studios, and was called the "proletariat" or "working man's" lot. Its films had a unique grit, pulse and vitality. Actress Geraldine Fitzgerald, under contract there for several years, once told this writer, "The other major studios made glamour films. At MGM, for instance, the stars extended their film selves into their own lives. You couldn't tell the Norma Shearer you saw up there on the screen from the Norma Shearer you met at a party. At Warners, it was kind of a slum. There was more realism."

It was the perfect environment for an idealistic young liberal Democrat actor, which is what Reagan was at the time.

Like the tree that grew in Brooklyn, the transplanted but adaptable Ronald Reagan bloomed in the extraordinary "asphalt jungle" of standing Warner sets—East Side tenements, speakeasies, courtrooms, jails and newspaper offices. Life on these mean streets was occasionally given respite at the Burbank studio's dusty, hot, all-purpose ranch at Calabasas about twenty miles away.

His second year there, 1938, found Reagan visible in no less than eight films and invisible in a ninth (*The Amazing Dr. Clitterhouse*, in which he returned briefly to being merely a voice on the radio). He was working, furthermore, with such players as Humphrey Bogart, Pat O'Brien, Dick Powell, Priscilla Lane, James Cagney and another newcomer named Edythe Marrenner, newly re-christened Susan Hayward. The alliterative Ronald Reagan was the rare movie actor then who was allowed to keep the name he was born with. (If Cary Grant had gone on to become President of the United States, would he have reverted to his real name, Archie Leach?)

Of Reagan's 1938 batch of appearances, most momentous was the farce from Broadway about Virginia Military Institute cadets titled *Brother Rat*, and not only because it turned out a hit. The film paired the sports-minded, romantically elusive twenty-seven-year-old actor with a pert, leggy contract starlet named Jane Wyman, who likewise was a long way from her mid-West home town, St. Joseph, Missouri, where she was born Sarah Jane Fulks on January 4, 1914.

Her geneology was clouded, probably by the studio publicity department which (even at Warners) never shrank from giving finishing school backgrounds to fair flowers of the Gowanus Canal. Was Jane Wyman's father the mayor of St. Joe, or the chief of detectives? She has claimed both, though of late she favors the latter occupation. Was she a radio singer before breaking into films? Yes, no, no and, most recently, yes. This much is certain: she was a blonde, big-eyed ex-chorus girl with a flair for comedy who, when she met Reagan, gave little indication that in the next decade she would become—in one of

The rented house in which Ronald Reagan grew up in Dixon, Illinois. Reagan himself has likened his youth to a Mark Twain idyll.

★ ★ ★

the medium's most startling transformations—the dignified, brunette first lady of the screen and winner of the Academy Award for her memorable portrayal of the pathetic deaf-mute in *Johnny Belinda* (1948). Aggressive and ambitious, she also would become the first Mrs. Ronald Reagan on January 26, 1940. It was her third marriage—Wyman was said to have been the last name of her mysterious, never-mentioned first husband, an obvious show biz choice over that of her second spouse and Reagan's immediate predecessor, middle-aged dress manufacturer Myron Futterman.

(Interestingly, in his 1965 autobiography Reagan incorrectly wrote that he met Jane Wyman in 1939. They met on the Warner lot in 1937. So much for ex-wives. But then—Wyman, too, has had trouble with dates. After more than four decades in which her birthdate was always given as January 4, 1914, she suddenly, and not too convincingly, announced in 1982 that it was actually January 5, 1917!)

After a short time, the new Mrs. Reagan, while confessing to being more cynical herself, remarked that her husband's most exasperating trait was always seeing the good in everyone and everything.

Their daughter, Maureen Elizabeth, was born on January 4, 1941 (also her mother's most frequently stated birthday), and in March, 1945, the Reagans adopted a twelve-hour-old boy they named Michael Edward.

Reagan made several late-1930s action "B"s portraying pulp hero "Brass" Bancroft, interspersed with solid "A"s such as *Dark Victory* (1939), starring studio queen Bette Davis, and shakier ones such as *Angels Wash Their Faces* (1939), with "oomph girl" Ann Sheridan and the Dead End Kids. There were three movies opposite Jane Wyman in 1940, *An Angel from Texas* and *Tugboat Annie Sails Again* plus the sequel *Brother Rat and a Baby*, wherein Wyman's smitten character spoke dialogue to Reagan that she later admitted could have been lifted from their real-life courtship: "You might as well back down, because I'm gonna get you."

Most significant that year, though, was *Knute Rockne, All American*, spotlighting Pat O'Brien as the beloved Notre Dame football coach and featuring Reagan as tragic running back hero George Gipp, a small but crucial role. To get it, Gipp admirer Ronald Reagan, aided by star O'Brien, had waged his first campaign.

Said Reagan, whose school years football-playing had served him well as "The Gipper," "Suddenly there were people on the lot greeting me who hadn't previously acknowledged my existence."

Pictures with Errol Flynn, Olivia de Havilland, Wallace Beery, Lionel Barrymore ensued. Neil Reagan enacted minor parts in some of his brother's films during this period, but eventually became an advertising executive. In the frugal Warner Brothers fashion, some early Reagan vehicles were remakes of story properties filmed previously by the studio.

And then the big one: *Kings Row* (1942), based on the popular, racy Henry Bellamann novel of dark doings in a small, turn-of-the-century American town. All departments excelled. "It was an astonishing film for its day," wrote Ted Sennett in his 1971 book *Warner Brothers Presents*, "containing little of the gentle, warmhearted folksiness that usually marked Hollywood's idea of Americana; instead there were strong hints (and sometimes more than hints) of sadism, madness and sexual hysteria." Add incest and bisexuality. Reagan, who once said that the story's milieu was "something I had more than slight acquaintance with" (!), won the prominent role of Drake McHugh, best friend of nominal lead Robert Cummings and local playboy whose legs were amputated needlessly by a sadistic doctor. His cry when he discovered what had transpired became the title of Reagan's autobiography: *Where's the Rest of Me?* Ann Sheridan was again Reagan's leading lady.

The North Dixon (Illinois) High School football team, 1926. Reagan is shown in the front row, fourth from left.

★ ★ ★

It is ironic that *Kings Row*, a production with a degenerate vision of grassroots America, remains the best-remembered film of the assertively wholesome American known as Ronald Reagan. It is also *his* favorite—"It made me a star."

Warners gave him a new contract ascending to $5,000 a week.

By this time Ronald Reagan and Jane Wyman (a few years away from a greater stardom than her husband) had become the inheritors of Mary Pickford's and Douglas Fairbanks' designation by an earlier generation as "Hollywood's Sweethearts."

The fan magazines could not get enough of this seemingly ideal young couple. Usually with the cooperation of their two subjects, they trumpeted, and sometimes perhaps trumped-up, the all-American appeal of "Ronnie" and "his Janie" and "Janie" and "her Ronnie" in articles headed "Happiness is a Thing Called You," "Yes! A Honeymoon Can Last in Hollywood IF—", "This Way, Mr. Stork" and "So Long, Button Nose," the latter piece sounding the 1942 call to arms for reservist Reagan as Second Lieutenant in the Cavalry. So unthinkable was their post-war divorce that stories on the pair such as their friend Louella Parsons' article, "Are They Haunted by Their Perfect Love?", continued to appear in the fan magazines well into Reagan's courtship of his second wife, MGM contract player Nancy Davis.

While her husband and so many others were in uniform, Jane Wyman sold war bonds, entertained at armed forces camps and at the Hollywood Canteen and managed to make one film after another.

There is no question that the aura of excitement about Ronald Reagan, Actor, created by the *Kings Row* attention was somewhat dissipated by his three-year service stint. In 1943, the army requested his return at service salary of $250 a month to his stuido, Warners, to film Irving Berlin's all-soldier stage revue *This is the Army*, the considerable proceeds from which went to Army Relief. He was then transferred to the first Air Force Motion Picture Unit, located at Culver City, California, which made hundreds of documentaries and training films, some with Reagan. But he was still off the commercial screen too long. His first film upon discharge, the dramatic *Stallion Road*, with Alexis Smith, was not released until 1947, and it was no smash.

Reagan's most successful features near the decade's close were in a lighter vein: *The Voice of the Turtle*, from the long-running Broadway romantic comedy and co-starring Eleanor Parker; *John Loves Mary*, introducing Patricia Neal to the screen in an adaptation of the stage farce; and *The Girl from Jones Beach*, opposite Virginia Mayo. In 1950 he again starred with Patricia Neal in the moving, British-filmed *The Hasty Heart* (another Broadway-based vehicle) and in 1951 with Ginger Rogers in the Ku Klux Klan exposé, *Storm Warning*.

Around then, the quality of his films began to decline. So did motion picture business in general, for two main reasons: 1) studios were forced by the government to give up ownership of their theaters, which had always assured them of showcases for their films; and 2) television was stealing movie audiences in growing and alarming number.

There was the now infamous *Bedtime for Bonzo* (1951), in which the future President of the United States played straight man to a chimpanzee. Four lesser productions co-starring Rhonda Fleming. *She's Working Her Way Through College* (1952), re-teaming him with Virginia Mayo in a musical version of the Broadway comedy *The Male Animal*. And his best film of this period, *The Winning Team* (1952), opposite Doris Day in the story of epileptic, alcoholic baseball great Grover Cleveland Alexander (Reagan).

After leaving Warner Brothers, he was reduced to doing films like *Cattle Queen of Montana* (1954), worth mention only because it permitted him to work with legendary lady Barbara Stanwyck. The low-budget *Hellcats of the Navy* (1957) found the actor vis-à-vis Nancy Davis, by then his wife. Although they acted together on television several times, this was their only joint big screen appearance.

Freshman Ronald Reagan (top row, third from left in glasses) is pictured with his dramatic fraternity in the Eureka (Illinois) College yearbook for 1928-29.

★ ★ ★

Reagan's 1949 divorce from Jane Wyman had been precipitated, it has been said most often, by his time- and attention-consuming interest in politics, even to the exclusion of his film career. By then, her film status had surpassed his, and she had an Oscar to prove it. He feels his road was probably mapped for him in the late 1940s when, as a last grasp for Hollywood superstardom, he asked studio boss Jack L. Warner to loan him to MGM to play—for his *Kings Row* director Sam Wood—one-legged baseball player Monty Stratton in *The Stratton Story*. Warner refused, and James Stewart triumphed in the part. Increasingly, Reagan preferred to talk (and talk) politics than movies. Except for one notable occasion, for Jane Wyman it was decidedly vice versa:

In their recent book *The People's Almanac No. 3*, David Wallechinsky and Irving Wallace claimed it was actually Reagan's love for his film *Kings Row* that clinched the marital breach. Seems he was in the habit of screening it for after-dinner guests, and the authors quoted a disaffected Wyman as saying, "I just couldn't stand to watch that damned *Kings Row* one more time."

A concerned, articulate and well-liked citizen, the young Roosevelt Democrat called Ronald Reagan had joined the Screen Actors Guild in 1938, became a "rabid" (his word) union man and in June, 1947, was elected President of the Screen Actors Guild. He served six terms in that capacity, from 1947 to 1952 and in 1960. His activities in office included fighting alleged Communist infiltration of the film industry and leading a strike to win residual rights for actors.

He met Nancy, the sedate daughter of erstwhile actress Edith Luckett and stepdaughter of conservative pioneer neurosurgeon Loyal Davis, when, as Guild President in 1949, he took her out to apprise the distressed young actress that it was another Nancy Davis whose name had been appearing on certain Communist lists. Born Anne Robbins on July 6, 1923 (or 1921, according to some sources), in New York City, Nancy had been raised in Chicago in "comfortable" (her word) circumstances. She hardly knew her real father, Kenneth Robbins, a New Jersey car salesman whom her Virginia-born mother divorced early.

After being graduated from Smith College, Nancy briefly modeled and acted on Broadway. In New York in the late 1940s, she dated a visiting Clark Gable often, and when Metro-Goldwyn-Mayer Studios in Hollywood sent for her, fan magazines slavered that it was probably because of the Gable connection. Certainly her friendships with MGM's two biggest male stars, Gable and Spencer Tracy (who had acted with her mother), didn't hurt her chances. She credits Tracy with arranging for famed "woman's director" George Cukor to guide her screen test.

She was signed by Metro. There, she garnered the most notice, not surprisingly, as the pregnant housewife in "message" picture producer Dore Schary's apotheosis, *The Next Voice You Hear* (1950), in which the voice of God interrupted radio programs everywhere to tell the world to clean up its act, or else. Perhaps the leading lady felt she would be helping the world to do that when, on March 4, 1952, she married Ronald Reagan.

On October 22, 1952, Patricia Ann Reagan was born to Ronald and Nancy, and on May 20, 1958, Ronald Prescott Reagan arrived. Family life took precedence over acting career to the second Mrs. Reagan. Her movie career was modest, anyway; she was a much plainer presence in her picture period than in her "Reagan red" high fashion Washington tenure. During her few years at MGM, the film capital's "glamour studio," Nancy's peculiar acting lot seemed to consist mainly of playing young matrons or schoolteachers.

In 1954 Reagan became host of television's *The General Electric Theater*, as well as national spokesman for G.E., and during the series' eight-year existence performed in many of its dramatic presentations. In 1964 he became host of, and sometimes actor in, TV's *Death Valley Days* for almost two seasons. *The Killers* (1964), containing his first real

The mid-1930s: Ronald Reagan when he was a sportscaster for Radio Station WHO in Des Moines, Iowa. Actress Joy Hodges met him there and, returning to Hollywood, got him his first agent in the film capital.

★ ★ ★

villain role in films, originally had been conceived as a television feature but proved too violent for that medium. It ended Ronald Reagan's movie career. Some felt that his political activism during his Hollywood years dissuaded certain studios from employing him as an actor.

Ostensibly, movie/TV-making had lost much of its appeal for the peripatetic Reagan, who claimed he found the demands of maintaining even an ebbing acting career "too confining." Nevertheless, amid the hysteria following the new President's shooting by John W. Hinckley, Jr., on March 30, 1981, Reagan, with typical vintage Warner Brothers flippancy, did crack, "If I'd gotten this much attention in Hollywood, I would never have left."

As the 1960s commenced he became more and more conservative and finally, circa 1964, announced that he had switched to the Republican party. Nancy Reagan explains: "By this time he knew he could no longer follow the Democratic leadership. As he tells it, the party had left him, he didn't leave the party. It no longer stood for the ideals and principles that had drawn him to it as a young man."

On November 8, 1966, he was elected Governor of California, serving two terms (eight years). "He took a bankrupt state and put it on a sound fiscal basis," boasted Nancy, who was never as appropriately cast in films as she was in the real-life role of politician's wife.

In 1980 the Republicans chose the ex-movie star as their candidate for President. The inevitable jokes followed.

Opposing independent Presidential candidate John Anderson: "Ronald Reagan is a man who made movies for 18th Century-Fox."

Film critic Gene Shalit: "Reagan will be the first President to deliver his State of the Union address while members of the House and Senate munch popcorn."

In spite of this, on January 20, 1981, Ronald Wilson Reagan was inaugurated fortieth President of the United States of America, succeeding incumbent Democratic candidate Jimmy Carter. He is the first divorced man to hold this office. At the time of his inauguration, soon to turn a virile seventy, he is also the oldest.

His children, of course, have since been thrust into the limelight, too. Thrice married daughter Maureen, after flings as actress, recording artist and talk show host, is interested in a political career as well. Michael both sells and races boats. Furthermore, on May 30, 1978, he and wife Colleen presented Reagan and Jane Wyman with their first grandchild, a boy named Cameron Michael. Patricia Ann Reagan, as Patti Davis, is an actress. Ronald Prescott Reagan is a ballet dancer.

Even the first Mrs. Ronald Reagan, a semi-retired Jane Wyman (who had gone on twice to marry and twice to divorce Hollywood musician Fred Karger), returned only months after Reagan's inauguration to star in the successful television series, *Falcon Crest*. For years, her main activities had been painting and working for the Arthritis Foundation. Now she has managed once again to surpass ex-husband Reagan. Her salary for a season's TV work is $770,000 while the President pulls down $200,000 plus expenses. In a total about-face from the pug-nosed war wife ideal and chatterbox of three decades ago, today she is a stately *doyenne du cinéma* who remains steadfastly, tastefully mum on the man with whom she launched a thousand movie magazine articles when they were "the perfect young American marrieds"—fighting for their country, fighting for their careers and, with sad and singular lack of success, fighting for their marriage.

When, in a bold headline on the pages of a 1942 issue of *Modern Screen*, Lieut. Ronald Reagan said "So Long, Button Nose" to wife Jane Wyman, it was at least as potent a recruiting boon as all the "Uncle Sam Wants You" posters and "Mom, I did it"/gung ho Hollywood join-up movies. He was saying "So long" for all the young men who were leaving loved ones for that "just war." She was every faithful girl "back home." Our fighting

In his film debut for the socially conscious Warner Brothers, Ronald Reagan (third from left) was given the lead of, appropriately, a radio announcer in a "B" called *Love Is on the Air* (1937). Also shown, from left: Willard Parker, William Hopper (Hedda's son) and Spec O'Donnell (rear).

★ ★ ★

forces just *had* to get these two back together again, just as the home front *had* to collect scrap metal and cooking grease.

Few got as far as the bottom line which revealed that poor eyesight had kept Capt. Reagan (his final rank) camped in his adopted home state of California for the duration. "Jane's Soldier" was even allowed to live at their Hollywood Hills home after a while.

Although Ronald Reagan's almost thirty-year film career has been called a minor one, and his own status that of a "B" movie actor, the considered truth is that neither is precisely true. He worked in several "B" movies early in his career, as did many newcomers then who went on to achieve importance in the industry, but he became a major star five years after his entrance into pictures. With the exception of (apologies to John Anderson) 20th Century-Fox, he made movies at all the top studios with many of Hollywood's fabled great, appearing, furthermore, in film versions of several of the most successful Broadway productions of the time. Female movie-goers liked his smiling, straightforward Irish charm, and males appreciated his breezy, often two-fisted image. When a role didn't demand too much depth, he was a convincing actor as well. There were reasons why he didn't reach the pantheon in pictures: the momentum lost during World War II service, his growing absorption in politics, studio resentment of his stands with the Guild.

No, Ronald Reagan's Hollywood years (1937-1965) are not to be dismissed lightly. If nothing else, they made the most powerful office in the world a reality for a man who might otherwise have lived out his time in pleasantly benign Mark Twain pastoralism.

Unless, of course, one believed *Kings Row*.

Ronald Reagan, his heavy thatch of hair re-styled by Warners make-up master Perc Westmore, sits for one of his earliest Hollywood portraits.

Lights! Camera! Action!

. . .We have ridden high together, you and I,
Into exalted channels of delight
Beyond the bugle call and battle cry
To paint our names in love upon the night.

ANN RICHARDS

The 1930S

Ronald Reagan, WHO sports announcer in Des Moines, has been placed under a term contract for pictures by Warner Brothers. The studio tested Reagan while he was here to scout the Chicago Cubs spring training at Catalina. He will report in June. William Meiklejohn Agency handled.

The Hollywood Reporter
April 15, 1937

★ ★ ★

They're on Their Way. . . Best Athlete: Ronald Reagan not only came to films from the field of sports broadcasting, but he knows whereof he speaks! The title of his latest film may be prophetic—it's *Going Places*, with Dick Powell, Anita Louise. . .

Movie Mirror
January, 1939

★ ★ ★

Hot dog! Yowsah, that indigestible little mutt is in the headlines again! Taking a tip from the Roosevelt party for King George and Queen Elizabeth, Her Royal Highness Anita Louise threw a wienie birthday shindig for Princess Pat Ellis. And—to top that other royal "dog day," the movie kings and queens answered the high command *à la* play togs. Tossing formality, glamour and diets to the winds, they had a royal time! Next day? Yes, both sunburn and tummyaches (for Anita, Pat, Lana Turner, Rosemary Lane, Dolores Del Rio, Wendy Barrie, Paula Stone and Jane Wyman and Ronald Reagan).

Picture Play
"Kings and Movie Queens Like Hot Dogs and Picnics, Too,"
September, 1939

★ ★ ★

Plenty of excitement for Jane Wyman these days what with her romance with Ronald Reagan sizzling and having Warner Bros. change her name to Janet to avoid confusion with Jane Bryan.

Movies
"In the Spotlight"
November, 1939

★ ★ ★

"HOLLYWOOD HOTEL"—A First National Picture

Reagan (center, carrying the "oo") had only a bit as a broadcaster in *Hollywood Hotel* (Warners, 1937), but out of it came a long friendship with powerful columnist Louella Parsons, whose radio show had inspired the film. Also shown, from left: Rosemary Lane, Dick Powell, Ted Healy, Allyn Joslyn, Hugh Herbert and Lola Lane.

★　★　★

Ronald Reagan, Jane Wyman, Perc Westmore and his wife, Gloria Dickson, seemed still amused over Slapsie Maxie Rosenbloom's antics as they left his Hollywood night club.

Movies
November, 1939

★ ★ ★

Frank McHugh, Jane Wyman, Ronald Reagan and Boris Karloff at the Hollywood Legion Stadium for the Screen Actors Guild mass meeting.

Silver Screen
"Topics for Gossip"
November, 1939

Irish descended actors Susan Hayward of Brooklyn and Ronald Reagan of Illinois—both recently signed by Warner Brothers—prepare to cool off in a Beverly Hills, California, swimming pool circa 1938.

★ ★ ★

The 1940S

The next thing Ronnie and Jane knew. . .there they were one night in the Tropics (Restaurant) and the middle of a proposal.

"He asked me what I was doing for the next fifty years," said Jane. "I said I had a date but nothing important."

Janie said it was about six months ago. Ronald said it was seven. Then they sat very straight, looked at each other wide-eyed and whispered, "That was September, more than a year ago."

They have been waiting ever since, film schedules being what they are, to get a vacation together, one long enough in which to get married and take a real honeymoon.

It being Jane's third marriage and Ronald's first, they recognize that they have certain snares to guard against. We even pointed out that his ceasing to be one of the few bachelors of the screen might affect Ronnie's popularity.

"You see what I'm giving up?" he said, turning sternly on Janie.

"But look what you're getting," Jane said.

Ruth Waterbury
"Wanted — One Honeymoon," by Ruth Waterbury
Movie Mirror, March, 1940

★ ★ ★

Ronald Reagan took his bride, Jane Wyman, dancing at the Grove on their first public appearance following their Palm Springs honeymoon.

Lois Svensrud
"Good News," by Lois Svensrud
Modern Screen, May, 1940

★ ★ ★

Mr. and Mrs. Ronald Reagan attended annual dinner dance at the Baltimore Hotel held by the Warner Brothers Club. Big feature of the evening was the running off of scenes showing stars blowing up in their lines in Warner films.

Movies
May, 1940

★ ★ ★

Sergeant Murphy (Warners, 1938) gave Reagan (second from left) the leading role of a cavalryman in the company of, from left: Henry Otho, Ben Hendricks, Jr., and Art Mix.

★ ★ ★

During early H'wood days he (Ronald Reagan) squired Susan Hayward. First love was a next-door neighbor whom he courted all thru school and planned to wed—until a Paris diplomat stole her heart! He wasn't bitter and kept an eye peeled for a sports-lover with humor. Janie (Wyman) was a hothouse flower, but love scenes in *Brother Rat* led to a 52-carat amethyst.

Modern Screen
1941

★ ★ ★

Pat O'Brien asked about-to-become-a-father-any-day-now Ronald Reagan whether he wanted a girl or a boy.

Ronnie wiped his forehead nervously, answered, "A *girl!* I wouldn't want any son of mine to go through what I'm going through, waiting for the baby to arrive!"

That's the first thing you notice about the Expectant Reagans. Ronnie is scared! Jane Wyman isn't. She is still the flip, wise-cracking young modern with apparently no more worry on her mind than a prom-trotting little co-ed.

It's not that Jane isn't excited about it. Good heavens, she even knits baby socks! But Jane, more than most young wives, has whipped the old-fashioned fears and bugaboos that usually herald the approach of the First Baby. She is a young modern, and she is facing motherhood in the proud way the modern girl faces just about anything these days.

Helen Ware
"This Way, Mr. Stork," by Helen Ware
Hollywood, January, 1941

★ ★ ★

Neither Ronnie or I were stars. We were both featured players making $500 a week. I wasn't a glamour queen and he wasn't a matinée idol. We were just two kids trying to get the breaks in pictures. . .

When I first met Ronnie I was a night club girl. I just had to go dancing and dining at the Troc or the Grove or some night spot every night to be happy.

Then Ronnie said to me, "Don't you ever swim, or play golf?" He was perfectly amazed that I didn't have the slightest conception about either.

We were both working on a picture called *Brother Rat*. We'd sit around the set and talk. But Ronnie was always going around with his college frat brothers. He never seemed to have time for girls. They were all enthused in sports.

One day the studio took Ann Sheridan, Ronnie and me out to the ice rink to pose for some publicity pictures. I couldn't even stand up on ice skates. Ronnie held me up long enough for pictures. He kidded me so terrifically about it, that Ann and I decided to skate or die. For two months we'd go out there every morning until we could actually figure skate.

That's how Ronnie and I began going together. Usually his frat brothers would be along, too. Instead of having a date with him alone, I'd be with four boys.

They took in all the sports—football, polo matches, horseback riding.

I didn't learn to swim until we went on our honeymoon to Palm Springs. I was so self-conscious I just couldn't let Ronnie teach me. So he hired a professional.

New girl in town Susan Hayward, two decades before her Academy Award for *I Want to Live!*, dates another Hollywood novice, fellow Warner contract player Ronald Reagan. The year: 1938.

★ ★ ★

Now I've taken up golf. You just can't keep me away from the club. I have a date with Mary (Livingstone) Benny this afternoon. Ronnie and I play together when we're both not working.

Jane Wyman
"Making a Double Go of It!", by Mary Jane Manners
Silver Screen, August, 1941

★ ★ ★

When he was in Philadelphia (on the Louella Parsons vaudeville tour in 1939), it took the police fifteen minutes to get him out of his hotel. When the women did get near him, they'd practically disrobe him. Several times he heard them ask, "Please, may I just touch you?" And they'd touch him whether he liked it or not and then breathe deeply and exhale an impassioned "Oh!" Even his hotel door became the knocking-board of every woman in town who could get past the clerk.

Ronnie didn't honestly enjoy this display. He was engaged to Jane, and besides such behavior bewildered him. It was the first time in his life that a public demonstration like that had happened to him. It did have one effect on Warners, though. It proved to the producers (who used to say, "Reagan for a real love scene? Impossible!") that he did have something that women admired. And it helped to bring about the current build-up of the new and romantic Ronald Reagan.

Jon Landon
"What! No Sex Appeal?", by Jon Landon
Motion Picture, October, 1941

★ ★ ★

Chronic honeymooners Ronnie Reagan and Jane Wyman are the town's greatest match-makers. Have married off all their pals but Eddie Albert.

Modern Screen
November, 1941

★ ★ ★

I don't know how I ever did it, but I was up to my neck in debt (when Ronnie and I decided to get married). And knowing the way Ronnie feels about debts, I decided the best thing to do was to pay every last living bill before the big event. After it was all over, I had exactly $500 to my name!

. . .Our system is so simple, it doesn't sound like anything. It's just that we save half of everything we make. . .

Ronnie has a phobia about bills. If a bill is ten days old, he starts having a fit. As a result, every bill is paid and out of the way by the 10th of each month.

Ronnie and I are a good balance for each other. While he is very practical in some respects, he goes overboard in others. For example, anyone can sell Ronnie *anything!* I don't think I'm tight, but over a period of years, I've come to learn the value of money and I insist on getting value received. I know how to cut corners and no one can sell me a

Warners got their money's worth out of Reagan, whom they put into one picture after another in the late 1930s. Above, center, Reagan in a scene from *Accidents Will Happen* (1938), also featuring, from left, Hugh O'Connell, Gloria Blondell, Dick Purcell and Addison Richards.

★ ★ ★

darned thing unless I'm convinced it is just what I want and that I'm getting it as cheaply as possible.

Jane Wyman
"Yes! A Honeymoon Can Last in Hollywood IF—"
by Virginia Wood
Screenland, November, 1941

★ ★ ★

Ann Sheridan and Ronald Reagan will co-star for the third time in Warners' *Casablanca*, with Dennis Morgan also coming in for top billing. Yarn of war refugees in French Morocco is based on an unproduced play by Murray Burnett and Joan Alison.

The Hollywood Reporter
January 5, 1942

★ ★ ★

Ronnie Reagan is ready and standing by. Just when his career and his personal life are rich with fulfillment, comes every indication that his services may be needed as a reserve member of the United States Cavalry. If he is called, the one hindrance may be the deficiency in his eyesight. Without his glasses, like Joan Bennett, Martha Scott and many others, Ronnie can't see clearly over five feet from him. Ronnie's adoring wife, Janey Wyman, isn't saying a word. But there's a hurt something in her face, as she goes gaily around Hollywood these days. Little Maureen Elizabeth, the baby Reagan, is too young and healthy to realize the drama that's going on around her.

Screenland
"Hot from Hollywood"
January, 1942

★ ★ ★

When Ronnie Reagan wore a turtle neck sweater on the *Juke Girl* set, Annie Sheridan gave him a terrific ribbing. She insisted on knowing whether the Hays Office had given their official permission!!!
("Sweater *girls*" were a censors' problem in 1942.)

Screenland
"Hot from Hollywood"
January, 1942

★ ★ ★

By her own rating, Jane's a cynical wench. ("It's an act," says her husband. "I *know*.") Battling her own way from an early age, she came up against all kinds and ended by taking very few on trust.
Then along came Reagan, loving his fellow men. Jane would eye him in wonder and exasperation. "I'd like to hear you knock someone, just for a change—"

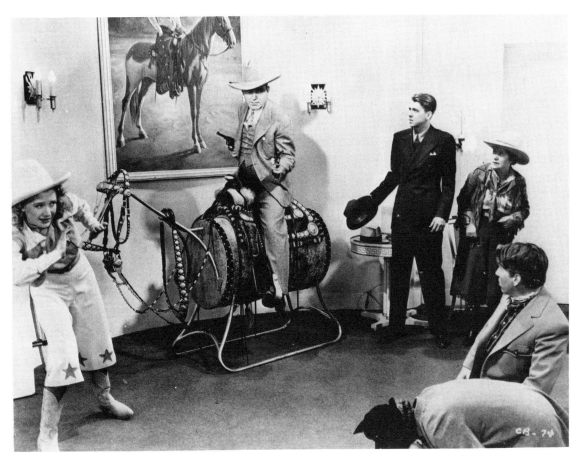

The Cowboy from Brooklyn (Warners, 1938) was the first of three movies that Reagan did with Pat O'Brien, who became a mentor and long-time friend. Pictured above are, from left: Priscilla Lane, O'Brien, Reagan, Emma Dunn and Johnnie Davis.

★ ★ ★

"Name him," said Ronnie, always obliging. Jane did. "Oh, he's okay. Always been swell to me. Don't believe everything you hear."

"But I didn't hear it, I know it."

"Well, maybe somebody conked him as a babe, and he never got over it. Anyway, what's it to us? Play golf."

. . .Says Jane, "I've never known his values to be anything but right. He sees and thinks straight."

For instance, the day Jane had a date to lunch with Joy Hodges. Joy phoned to the restaurant that she couldn't make it. A director who wanted Jane for a part she was eager to play sat down at her table. They discussed pros and cons through most of the afternoon.

Next day the papers had it. "Jane Wyman was seen lunching with so-and-so. Wonder if the Reagans are breaking up?"

She showed it to Ronnie. "What do you think of that?"

"I think it's funny." She kissed him.

"What's that for?"

"I think you're lovely."

Kaaren Pieck
"Non-Stop Honeymoon," by Kaaren Pieck
Modern Screen, February, 1942

★ ★ ★

Chief among Hollywood pipe collectors is Ronald Reagan, who was amassing the implements for a hearty smoke screen long before he met Jane Wyman. After they were married and she moved into the Reagan apartment, the little woman continued to encourage Ronnie, and to gloat as happily as he did whenever a particularly exciting specimen was added. She conferred with him upon the exact spot in the Reagan den to be occupied by each new pipe.

This happy state continued until Miss Maureen Elizabeth Reagan came home from the hospital with her mother. The Reagans didn't want to move, but they *had* to have a nursery.

You guessed it: the younger generation took over the den, and Ronnie's pipes got deported to his studio dressing room.

Fredda Dudley
"Pipe Collector," by Fredda Dudley
Hollywood, 1942

★ ★ ★

Trying to juggle marriage and an acting career at the same time is an occupation that rates as one of Hollywood's most hazardous. Few actresses have accomplished this feat without smashing either home-life or professional standing. It takes steadiness and a sure grasp of one's own capabilities.

That's the trick Jane Wyman is attempting right now. To avoid disaster in either direction, she must look at herself with critical detachment. But when she does that, she sees double, or triple. She sees several Jane Wymans: Mrs. Ronald Reagan — the mother of little Maureen Elizabeth Reagan — the Warner Brothers "cutie" who gets more fan mail each day — and a fourth hazy figure that might be Jane Wyman, dramatic actress.

Brother Rat (Warners, 1938), from the John Monks, Jr.–Fred F. Finklehoffe stage farce, featured Reagan, Jane Wyman and Wayne Morris. Ronnie and Janie were sweethearts, on screen and off.

★ ★ ★

A turning point in her husband's career has given Jane new ideas about her own. Reagan has just graduated from a long series of comedy and light melodramatic roles to a dramatic part in *Kings Row*. Established as a comedienne, Jane has developed the clown's traditional yearning to play Hamlet—or Ophelia, in this case. She knows her designs will probably run up against studio opposition. Her experience as a radio singer makes her still more valuable as a comedienne, because of Hollywood's reviving interest in musicals.

Is she wise to complicate an already complex task with new ambitions? Jane has her own misgivings: "Maybe two serious careers would be too much in a single family," she argues with herself. "Perhaps it is better to let Ronnie play drama and let me work at having fun. It keeps a happy balance in our family life." For the sake of both career and marriage, she will have to decide soon which one of the many Jane Wymans is most important.

Screen Guide
"Who Does Jane Wyman Think She Is?"
June, 1942

★ ★ ★

It's Jane's war now. It had been just The War, till one day she got home from the studio, and there was this funny expression on Ronnie's face—Now it's Jane's war.

She'd read about it. She'd worked for the Red Cross and been wakened by anti-aircraft fire and entertained the boys at army camps. She'd seen Ronnie's sick face bent over a picture of the small swollen bodies of children starved to death in Poland. "This," said the war-hating Reagan between set lips, "would make it a pleasure to kill." That night he'd stood a little longer beside the crib of Button-nose the Second, who'd inherited both the nose and the name from her mother.

She'd known Ronnie would go, that he'd probably have enlisted after Pearl Harbor if he hadn't been a member of the Cavalry Reserve. . .

One day at the beginning of April she came home from 20th Century-Fox where she was making *Footlight Serenade*—

She came home mad. It had been one of those days when everything went wrong. She stormed upstairs to spill it to Ronnie, her safety valve. He generally laughed. For some reason, he thought her tantrums funny. Let him laugh. She'd get it off her chest anyway—

Ronnie was lying down. He'd had one of his rare days off from *Desperate Journey*. The letter had arrived after Jane left. He'd spent the hours waiting, fighting a sense of oppression, hoping something would happen to give him an idea how best to break the news—

She burst in and slammed her hat on the bed. "Has *this* been a day! So help me, Ronnie, nothing can happen to touch what's happened to me today—"

He didn't laugh. He looked at her, and there was this funny expression on his face. Before he said it, she knew what he was going to say. "Sorry, honey, because here's something else—"

He gave her the notice, calling Second Lieutenant Ronald Reagan of the United States Cavalry Reserve to active duty on April 20th at Fort Mason, California. A piece of white paper that changed their lives. You can expect and expect a thing to happen but, till it hits

The leading players in *Brother Rat* (Warners, 1938), from left: William Tracy, Johnnie Davis, Eddie Albert, Larry Williams, Ronald Reagan, Wayne Morris, Jane Wyman and Priscilla Lane. It was Reagan's first real film hit.

★ ★ ★

you, it's as if you'd never expected it at all. Now it's real, she thought. Now it's Ronnie's war and mine.

Cynthia Miller
"So Long, Button-Nose," by Cynthia Miller
Modern Screen, July, 1942

★ ★ ★

Fri., May 15th: Cynthia Miller's lunch-time interview with Jane Wyman at the Beverly Hills Brown Derby was the high spot on the calendar today. Jane breezed into the eatery wearing a tailored suit and sun glasses and clutching a handful of business letters. She'll personally handle the Reagans' finances while Ronnie's gone. Showed us a letter she had from Ronnie only this morning. It was full of the old Reagan pep and enthusiasm. There were long passages about Dr. Margaret Chung, the famous American-born woman surgeon he met in San Francisco. Dr. Chung, who is known as "Mother" to 475 leading American flyers, has "sons" winging over Germany, Australia, China and every far corner of the world. Ronnie can't be a "son," but he hopes she'll accept him into a separate unit she formed for friends of flyers. If he makes the grade, he'll be in the company of people like Helen Hayes, Bob Young and Cornelia Otis Skinner.

Sylvia Kahn
"Good News," by Sylvia Kahn
Modern Screen, July, 1942

★ ★ ★

The air corps wings Jane (Wyman) proudly displays are the real thing. She has been commissioned a colonel in the air corps and when she's in uniform, Ronald, a second lieutenant, has to salute Jane—his superior officer. Jane is eligible for active service in the public relations office now.

Screen Guide
"We're in the Army Now!"
Screen Guide, August, 1942

★ ★ ★

Jane Wyman and wee daughter are probably the happiest people in town since husband and daddy Ronald Reagan has been temporarily sent back to Burbank to make Government shorts.

Cal York
"Inside Stuff," by Cal York
Photoplay, September, 1942

★ ★ ★

LETTERS TO THE EDITOR
Ronald Reagan Recruits for Uncle Sam: Why do magazines give so much credit to Gable, Stewart and Power for joining up and forget about Ronald Reagan? After all, Reagan had

Tyro Susan Hayward, left, had her largest role to date in *Girls on Probation* (Warners, 1938), although Ronald Reagan and Jane Bryan had the leads. Also pictured: Joseph Crehan.

★ ★ ★

just reached stardom when he joined, and I know some boys who enlisted when Reagan did because they said that if he could give up so much, they could, too.

Alma Harten
34 East 68th St., N.Y.C.
Screen Guide, 1942

★ ★ ★

Poor Lieut. R. ordered an expensive gift for J., only to be told by the shop-keeper that his charge account had been closed when he entered the service! His pockets revealed a mere $2.24. "Charge it to my wife," said he. "She's still in pictures!"

Modern Screen
January, 1943

★ ★ ★

It's nine months now since Ronald Reagan said, "So long, Button-nose" to his wife and baby, and went off to join his regiment. Button-nose the First—Jane Wyman to you—has adjusted herself to the new way of life. She's run into lots of girls who've lost their guys to the army, and they all react the same way. You go through agonies beforehand. You go through the wrenching agony of good-by. You go back alone to your house with the same enthusiasm you'd take into a morgue. After that, nothing else is quite so bad.

Keeping busy helps. Jane had no trouble that way. There was the house and the baby and war work and all the little things Ronnie used to take care of, not to mention her job. Going back to the studio was almost as tough as going back to the house. She'd catch herself looking for him as she turned a corner of the lot, listening for his, "Hi, kid," or his idiotic "Mrs. Reagan, I presume."

At Ronnie's request, she went out to one of the staging areas to sing for the boys about to be sent overseas. "Tangerine" she sang, and "He's 1–A in the Army" and "Not Mine" and "I Said No." And would have sung all night, had army regulations permitted. . . She opened the stamp and bond-selling booth outside the theater that was showing *Kings Row* and her own picture, *My Favorite Spy*. Phil Harris was on the stage. By arrangement, she broke into his show, explained why she was there and suggested that if the folks wanted to say hello as they left, she'd be glad to take care of their spare cash. . .

Not long after an order came through from Washington, transferring Ronnie from cavalry to air force. It meant being stationed near home. Before gas rationing, Jane would hop into her car after work on Saturday and stay with him till Sunday night. He could get home for an occasional evening or week-end. That was the nice part. . .

Naturally, when Ronnie comes home, it's a holiday but a quiet one. Just being there, just having him there, is enough. He's a very sentimental guy, says his wife, and like an old dog about this house they moved into only three weeks before he left. You can sort of see him curling himself up, laying his head on his paws and feeling good. It's the place he belongs to, the place where he wants to live and die.

Ida Zeitlin
"My Soldier," by Ida Zeitlin
Modern Screen, January, 1943

★ ★ ★

Going Places (Warners, 1938) was a prophetic title for Reagan, shown above second from right. Also pictured, from left: Larry Williams, Thurston Hall, Anita Louise and Minna Gombell. Reagan's good friend Dick Powell, not present, was top-billed.

★ ★ ★

With Ronnie in the army, Jane Wyman's been touring; helping in any way she can. Stars like Merle Oberon, Martha Raye, Edward G. Robinson and Al Jolson have gone overseas to cheer troops. Others have taken part in 220 special broadcasts for Gov. agencies such as the War and Treas. Depts. and Navy.

Modern Screen
February, 1943

★ ★ ★

Brother Rat very definitely was a turning point in Jane Wyman and Ronald Reagan's lives. It brought them professional success and personal happiness. On location at the San Diego Military Academy, when day and work were done, they used to stroll along the Coronado beach. In the beginning — the first night — they did this because they had nothing better to do. That was 1938, but neither Jane nor Ronald has had eyes for anyone else since then, except — during the last year or two — their Maureen Elizabeth.

"Fearless"
"The Truth About Location Loves," by "Fearless"
Photoplay, April, 1943

★ ★ ★

Women used to hesitate to admit that they dressed to please men. Today, they brag about it. They plan their lives and their wardrobes to please them. They want to look their best and be their gayest when he (sweetheart, husband, brother or son) comes home on leave. Jane Wyman, appearing in *Princess O'Rourke*, selected the clothes on these pages because she knew hubby, Lt. Ronald Reagan, would approve. The clothes are all colorful and casual and they'll compliment his uniforms — whether they are Navy blues, pinks or khaki G.I.'s.

Holly Wood
"Furlough Fashions," by Holly Wood
Motion Picture, June, 1943

★ ★ ★

Reagans' Roost: their Hollywood Hills English farmhouse. Designed for comfort, the Reagan living room is done in chintzes, crashes and fine reproductions. Accessories make a room. Jane uses them in moderation and in excellent taste. The china, the lamps, the English prints, all add interest. The master bedroom is a masterpiece. Done in organdy, chintz and cotton, it's crisp, cool-looking and utterly charming. The nursery is of modest proportions and modestly decorated but definitely fresh and feminine.

Motion Picture
July, 1943

★ ★ ★

Future stars Ronald Reagan and Lana Turner are shown above (second and third from right) watching the horses at Kellogg's Ranch, where their studio filmed many of their outdoor productions. The year is 1938, and other young Warner contract players pictured are, from left: Vicki Lester, Kenny Baker, Anna Johns, Dick Foran and Marie Wilson.

After finishing his role of corporal in *This is the Army*, Lt. Ronald Reagan's back with the Air Force. His mail's doubled since joining up; fans are clamoring for more of Janie on the screen!

Modern Screen
August, 1943

★ ★ ★

Hollywood opening of *This is the Army*, which he attended with his wife, Jane Wyman, was big moment for Ronnie (Reagan) who was given assignment by the army to play a part in it. Troops in camouflaged snipers' uniforms provided atmosphere at premiere of picture, the first Ronnie has made since he joined the army more than a year ago, and the last he is likely to make until the war is entirely over.

Movie Life
November, 1943

★ ★ ★

Captain Ronald Reagan, former movie star and now serving with the Army Air Force First Motion Picture Unit, today will light the new victory torch of Southern California's women at war.

He will report for duty at the Examiner Recruiting Headquarters, 424 West Sixth Street, to welcome the first contingent of women to apply for enlistment in the service of their country as a WAC, a WAVE, a SPAR or MARINE.

He will remind them they must replace men before aid can be released for a sweetheart, a husband, brother and son "over there" and thus bring him home the more quickly.

And Captain Reagan will autograph booklets on the branch of service chosen by the applicants and answer questions about that service.

Los Angeles Examiner
January 14, 1944

★ ★ ★

Capt. Ronald Reagan, on a short leave, spent his in Hollywood, went to the Canteen with his wife, Jane Wyman, who works there regularly.

Movie Life
February, 1944

★ ★ ★

Not far from the beach (where Reagan was a lifeguard) nestles the Dixon Insane Asylum. Occasionally an inmate would break out. Nobody's pressure went up. "One of our nuts got loose," the authorities would phone. "If you see him, pick him up."

Reagan is pictured with John Litel in *Secret Service of the Air* (Warners, 1939), the first of his four "B" movie appearances as pilot-turned-secret serviceman "Brass" Bancroft.

But one day the phone call held a more urgent note. Two Negroes and a white, all homicidal maniacs, had escaped. "They're bad ones," came the warning. "Watch out for them."

As Ronnie crossed the river that night for a date at a cabin party, he could see, among the wooded hills, the lights of the searchers. They were still searching two hours later when, alone, he had to paddle his canoe back, beach it and cover a stretch of dense woodland to get to his car. Not only did he cock his gun — he kept his thumb on the hammer, pulled the trigger. Every shadow held a threat, every leaf that stirred a lurking danger. It was the longest walk he ever took.

Anticlimax. Nothing happened. No mad eyes gleamed through the darkness, no mad claws clutched. He got home feeling a little shaken, slightly foolish and intensely relieved.

On a Chicago bus that fall his eye hit a newspaper story. A lunatic had attacked a woman and knifed two cops before being cornered. "He and two Negro companions," the story concluded, "escaped from the Dixon Insane Asylum last August."

Ida Zeitlin
"Ronald Reagan, Part II," by Ida Zeitlin
Modern Screen, 1944

★ ★ ★

After Ronnie left Jane and H'wood for Army, his fan mail swelled to second place on Warner lot. Errol Flynn, 1st in hearts of mash-note-writers, beat him by a couple of stacks.

Modern Screen
April, 1944

★ ★ ★

Acting is something he did in another life. His mind has no room for it now. Morning or noon, midnight or five o'clock, he's buried deep in the war.

The war's also of paramount importance to Jane. As you know from *Modern Screen*, she's poured her time and strength into war work, in Hollywood and out. But like most of us, she needs occasional surcease from the subject. Ronnie doesn't.

Jane has served a long apprenticeship at Warners. Time was when her recognition as a star would have called for cheers and whoopee from Ronnie. His own brand of whoopee, to be sure. Nothing ostentatious on the surface, but definitely steamed up inside.

As it was, he only said: "That's swell, Janie. It's about time. By the way, did you see that story on page 3 of the *Times?* It says—"

Jane is devoted to her brother-in-law. But when Ronnie's home of an evening, Neil's arrival sends her heart into her boots. Argument is meat and drink to them both, and they'd rather argue about the war than sit down to a pre-Pearl Harbor steak. As for trying to break them up, a butterfly might as well try to break up a couple of bears. They don't even hear her.

"Okay, gentlemen. I'm going to bed," she said bitterly one night.

If she thought they'd stop her, she had another think coming. Their voices rose to the bedroom, where she was trying to read. Suddenly the sense of her injuries overwhelmed her. Down went the book. Was she a woman or a worm? She rang for Nanny.

"Will you please ask Mr. Reagan to come up?"

"Put 'em up, Tip O'Neill!" Actually, Ronald Reagan appears here in a close-up from *Secret Service of the Air* (Warners, 1938), wherein he enacted the two-fisted hero.

"Which one?"

"Both of them."

"Moon," she began firmly, "you've got to go home."

"Why, what did I do?"

Her firmness broke into a wail. "First you won't let me get a word in edgewise, and now I can't even read. Don't *look* at me that way," she blubbered. "I *know* nothing matters but the war. But *somewhere* there are beautiful people who *do* talk about something else *some of the time—*"

By now Ronnie's arms were around her, and the rest was smothered in his chest. It was just as well that she missed the glance exchanged by her menfolk. "Women!" said the glance.

Ida Zeitlin
"Even in the Best of Families. . .", by Ida Zeitlin
Modern Screen, April, 1944

★ ★ ★

You remember the old (Kipling) line about the colonel's lady and Judy O'Grady being sisters under the skin? Well, not only is it true, but it applies to captain's ladies, also. Jane Wyman Reagan, for one. She's just plain folks. She was born folks. Sarah Jane Folks (Fulks), to be precise. And she comes from Missouri and has to be shown. . . A realist, Janie. But such a nice, romantic realist, as her captain could tell you.

She started out with big ideas and small jobs, such as hairdressing, manicuring, modeling, switchboard operating, stenographing. All of which gets chalked up to experience that makes for more roundness, a little more sympathy, just possibly a little more soul. She had a sense of humor to begin with. That helped. "I was born in St. Joseph, Missouri. Me and Jesse James."

She swears she had to work to get him (Ronnie) to ask her to say yes. He liked her fine, but he wasn't awfully quick at falling in love. Anyway, that's her story. He did her a lot of good, too. Kind of gentled her. They go together like—well, to coin a phrase, like June and moon.

And there's Maureen Reagan, who wheedles the ears right off them, and they love it. . . She's a big girl now—all of three last January fourth. . .

Altogether, it was a nice life, back before the war. And it'll be a nice life again. Ronald sprawling happily all over the house, talking loudly about his own excellent taste because he chose it—and will you have the kindness to look at that view! And there'll be Jane blues-singing at the top of her voice because she likes to blues-sing. And Maureen just being Maureen, sure she's positively irresistible, which is okay, because she is. They all are.

Screen Romances
"Captain's Lady," May, 1944

★ ★ ★

With eyes only for each other, Jane Wyman and Captain Ronald Reagan keep stacking up proof that they're one of Hollywood's most happily married couples. . . One of film colony's first war wives (Ronnie went into service in April, 1942), Jane is also one of the busiest, what with bond tours, war work, looking after Maureen and the Reagan dogs,

Bette Davis has said that her favorite movie was *Dark Victory* (Warners, 1939), in which she played a dying playgirl and Reagan appeared as one of her swains. Davis boasts that she did not vote for Reagan for President of the U.S.

Scotch and Soda. And making movies, too, of course. Her next is *The Doughgirls*, filming of the Broadway smash hit.

Movie Life
July, 1944

★ ★ ★

It was Ronnie's easy friendship which attracted me to him first. Everyone liked him and it seemed to me that he liked nearly everyone. I began to analyze what it was in *me* that *he* liked. . .and to try and have more of it!

Jane Wyman
"Happiness is a Thing Called You"
by Jane Wyman and Helen Louise Walker
Movieland, July, 1944

★ ★ ★

In the days when Ronnie was not yet Captain Reagan, and when Janey was still a bride, the two of them were members of a personal appearance troupe appearing at the Chicago Theater. When the stars were entertained at a luncheon by a local advertising club, the groom was unable to attend because of a sore throat. The toastmaster, explaining the fact, made a heavy-handed attempt at humor:
    "His bride will tell you about him," he said. "The former Mr. Reagan is now Mr. Jane Wyman, you know!"
    Janey popped to her feet. "Please, people," she said, her brown eyes blazing. "I hope you'll skip that introduction. Why, gosh—Ronnie would just break my neck if he thought I'd take a bow on a statement like that!"
    Well, Janey still has her pretty neck, hasn't she?

Dee Ofstie
"Off the Record. . .", by Dee Ofstie
Movieland, October, 1944

★ ★ ★

It's Ronnie who's Irish, but Jane who's moody. Up in the clouds or down in the depths of gloom—never a happy medium, no matter how she tries, and she tries hard—
    "My husband and I," says Jane, "are like Scotch and Soda (their dogs)."
    Soda takes after Ronnie, Scotch after her. One day Scotch got mad and started snapping at Soda. For a moment, Soda watched him tolerantly—"Pipe down, brother, pipe down." When that didn't work, he lifted his paw and laid it quietly on his brother's nose. It worked like a charm. Scotch subsided, Soda removed the paw and they trotted off together in brotherly love.
    "And if those aren't my husband's tactics, I'll eat my hat," remarked Jane out loud.
    Few people are as honest with themselves as Jane. Few people see their faults so clearly. If things at the studio upset her, she gripes about them at home. She flies off the handle. She knows she shouldn't, but she does. When Ronnie's around, he tries to calm her down. But she doesn't want to be calm, she wants to storm—
    "You don't know what things are like. You've been away too long."

Among Ronald Reagan's most prestigious early films was *Dark Victory* (Warners, 1939), starring Bette Davis (Right) and featuring Geraldine Fitzgerald. Reagan played an imbibing beau of Bette's.

"Things like that don't change. It's just a question of diplomacy."

Time passes, and she cools off — realizing that Ronnie has his own problems, that it can't be fun to come home on a week-end pass and listen to her beef. Her conscience smites her. Jane's temper is warm, but not nearly so warm as her heart.

Ida Zeitlin
"Nutty But Nice," by Ida Zeitlin
Modern Screen, October, 1944

★ ★ ★

Strange as that seems in Hollywood, those ever-lovin' Reagans — Ronald and Jane — never get tired of each other!

Kay Hardy
"Hollywood Chatterbox," by Kay Hardy
Screen Romances, December, 1944

★ ★ ★

Suddenly in *Doughgirls*, she set the screen on fire. "So what's the difference?" she wants to know. "When you're not a star, they call you Jane. When you're a star, they call you Miss Wyman. I'd rather be Jane." But don't think she hates it. It's good to travel *up* for a change. It's good just to travel, like she says. "It's not so much whether you're going to the top or way to the bottom, as long as you're moving. But standing still, you stifle." Symptoms of her new renown are evident. Her ever lovin' Reagan got a week-end pass, and they took themselves off to a restaurant for a good meal. She's a good kid, of course, but when it comes to cooks, give him Dave Chasen's. Anyhow, after the main dish, Ronnie went to make a phone call, and Jane ordered coffee. "For Mr. Wyman, too?" the waiter asked. She choked right in his face. Boy, guess *that* meant Wyman had arrived. And when Reagan got back, she gloated. He only grinned. "Just wait till I get out of this uniform, pipsqueak. I'll show you some stuff." She admits that he no doubt will.

Screen Album
1944

★ ★ ★

When rumor started that all was not well with the Reagans, Ronnie got to the base of it, found culprit and warned him that, uniform or not, he'd throttle him if he didn't retract statements.

Modern Screen
January, 1945

★ ★ ★

Ronald Reagan and character actors John Gallaudet and Stuart Holmes take a chance in *Code of the Secret Service* (Warners, 1939), the second in Reagan's low-budget "Brass" Bancroft series.

The Ronald Reagans were kept busy signing and signing autographs at the celebrity-packed (1945) Ice Follies preme. A swell pair—Jane and Ronald.

May Mann
"Going Hollywood with May Mann"
Screen Stars, January, 1945

★ ★ ★

Captain Ronald Reagan and his wife, Jane Wyman, obliged autograph hunters waiting in front of Ciro's for just such a break.

Movie Story
"Movie Story's Gossip," January, 1945

★ ★ ★

Fans' Forum
First Prize Winner: $10.00. Recently I read that 1944 had the largest divorce rate in history and I overheard the remark that three-fourths of them were Hollywood divorces. It brought to my mind the really few Hollywood marriages that do last. These few were people like the Nelson Eddys, Fred MacMurrays, Ray Millands and Fredric Marches—marriages where only one of the couple is in pictures. But I'd like to take my hat off to a couple who have proven that a marriage between two equally popular stars can last. They are the lovable Reagans. Ronald and Jane were married when they both were doing only small parts. When Ronald began to get better roles, professional jealousy did not come between them. And now Jane is at last getting the parts she deserves, roles worthy of her talents. Ronnie went into the Army when he was at the peak of his career and yet he is still one of the most popular actors in Hollywood. This was proven by the fact that he was chosen sixth in a recent popularity poll although he hasn't starred in a picture for two years. It makes me feel good to see the Reagans together and I know that in the years to come, little Maureen will have plenty of reasons to be proud of her parents.

Dickie Cline
Lancaster, Pa.
Screenland, June, 1945

★ ★ ★

There should be a few red faces amongst the "friends" of Jane Wyman and Ronald Reagan. While Ronnie's been doing a bang-up job for Uncle Sam, Jane made several mysterious trips out of town. Immediately tongues began to wag. Was something wrong in the Reagan household? Jane and Ronnie smiled wryly to themselves and said nothing. Now the truth can be told. Jane was hunting for a little brother to adopt for daughter Maureen. He is now in his new home, and his name is Michael Edward Reagan.

Screenland
"Hot from Hollywood," July, 1945

★ ★ ★

Reagan did battle with crooks and the obstreperous Dead End Kids in *Hell's Kitchen* (Warners, 1939), but won Margaret Lindsay for his trouble.

Re the adoption of Michael Edward Reagan:

One of Jane's best friends said in amazement, when Jane sighed and admitted that finding just exactly the right baby (to adopt) was a serious and difficult matter, "Heavens, Jane, your first child is such a success that I can't see why you simply don't *have* another of your own."

The answer to that is simple:

Like all Army couples, Jane and Ronnie have had to figure financial angles carefully, because, before the war began, they had bought a rather expensive hilltop house and—with Ronnie in uniform after all the papers were signed—Jane wanted to keep up payments.

So Jane's earning power before the camera has been important; she hasn't felt that she could take out the precious time that having a baby would demand.

Then there was another, more important reason for adopting a baby. Jane has said hundreds of times that she and Ronnie are two of the luckiest people in the world; they were lucky to find one another, lucky to have a button-nose like Maureen, and lucky in their careers. In a world where there are many children who never have proper care or love and who never know real home life, Jane thinks it is important for people like herself and Ronnie to add, from the outside, to their family—and then to regard the newcomer as flesh of their flesh, bone of their bone.

Fredda Dudley
"Those Reagans!", by Fredda Dudley
Modern Screen, July, 1945

★　★　★

Question: Who do you think has the most beautiful figure in Hollywood?

Answer: I wouldn't throw rocks at Jane Wyman. (If Ronnie's listening in, I'm only kidding.)

Jack Carson
"Popping Questions at Jack Carson," by Helen Hover
Motion Picture, October, 1945

★　★　★

The Ronald Reagan formula for a happy marriage calls for a dress-up date at least once a week.

Rita Hayworth
"Let's Gossip with Rita Hayworth (Guest Editor)"
Motion Picture, November, 1945

★　★　★

Will there be room for both the male wartime and male peacetime stars in movies, Hollywood is asking? During the war an amazing number of men stars burst into being: Van Johnson, Peter Lawford, Robert Walker, Tom Drake, Cornel Wilde, Gregory Peck, John Hodiak and many more. But already out of uniform or soon to don mufti again are such peacetime favorites as: Jimmy Stewart, Tyrone Power, Robert Montgomery, Henry

Reagan made the second of four appearances with "Oomph Girl" Ann Sheridan in *Angels Wash Their Faces* (Warners, 1939), the title for which was inspired by the James Cagney hit of the previous year, *Angels with Dirty Faces*. Frankie Thomas (above) was in support.

Fonda, Clark Gable, Ronald Reagan, Lon McCallister, Donald O'Connor, Gene Kelly, Victor Mature, Wayne Morris and many other golden boys. Yes, it's the problem of whether it is to be the new FF's or the old Famous Faces — or both! Just to complicate the problem let us add that there are in total 1,500 GI's returning from overseas to the acting ranks. How to get all of them back before the cameras is of course Question Number One — and the answer must be Yes!

"Fearless"
"Hollywood's Talking About — ", by "Fearless"
Photoplay, December, 1945

★　★　★

Jane Wyman and Ann Sothern are two of the happiest lassies in town these days, for it's no longer Capt. Ronald Reagan and Lt. Robert Sterling — just Ronnie and Bob, on the Warner and Metro lots. Both returnees will probably have their first pictures set any day now.

Movieland
"So Proudly We Hail," December, 1945

★　★　★

Nobody ever chats to Jane (Wyman) three minutes without her mentioning Ronnie Reagan.

Screen Album
1945

★　★　★

The Payoff. Ronald Reagan probably won't appreciate my telling this, but it's too good to keep. It seems that he and the little woman, Jane Wyman, having planned an afternoon at the Santa Anita races, failed to agree about the best bet in the sixth race. Jane, forced to cancel her own plans by a sudden studio call, nevertheless urged Ronnie to go — and gave him a ten-dollar bill, with explicit instructions to bet it "on the nose" of her sixth race choice. Ronnie was so convinced her horse couldn't win that he disregarded the instructions. To his embarrassment, her nag came in winner by nearly two lengths. "What did you do?" I asked him. "The same thing any husband who values domestic peace would have done," he answered. "I made good out of my allowance — at nine to one!"

Jimmie Fidler
"Jimmie Fidler in Hollywood"
Screen Romances, April, 1946

★　★　★

In *Smashing the Money Ring* (Warners, 1939), the third entry in the "Brass" Bancroft series, the following players figured prominently, from left: Eddie Foy, Jr., Margot Stevenson, Reagan and William Davidson.

The Reagans no longer address daughter as Murmur. She insists on correct Maureen. Their friends call her The Character.

Movie Stars Parade
"Passing Parade," April, 1946

★ ★ ★

Lieutenant in Officers' Reserve Corps pre-war, Ronnie Reagan was called to colors in '42. Back at Warners he'll be *Will Rogers*. Has new adopted son.

Movie Stars Parade
April, 1946

★ ★ ★

Always a thoughtful guy, the war hasn't made Ronnie less so, and Jane's kept pace with him. Out of the last six years he brought a credo: That we have one great responsibility—to stop war. There are forces at work that don't want it stopped. It's up to us to fight them. Up to *you*, says Ronald—not your neighbor or your congressman or the fellow who's got more time. You'll never give time to anything more important.

He's fighting through the American Veterans' Society, through speeches to clubs and civic bodies, all dealing with the plot against the peace. He's fighting with all his heart and strength, and sometimes with a touch of desperation—

"Now it's a simple choice," says Ronnie. "Either you leave your children a world at peace, or no world at all"—

Abigail Putnam
"Peace, It's Wonderful!", by Abigail Putnam
Modern Screen, July, 1946

★ ★ ★

Thousands of nice young couples all over this country have two jobs in one family, and they do all right. They adjust to it and one another because they want to get along—more than any other thing in the world. There's no reason why two actors can't do the same if they're in love and don't start taking themselves big. Even if Ronnie and I ever started getting that way I think the kids would stop us, because I assure you that both of us combined can't top our Maureen for pure hamming.

Jane Wyman
"Louella O. Parsons in Hollywood"
Los Angeles Examiner
July 4, 1946

★ ★ ★

I still remember our first date. We had a dinner date and went to a Sonja Henie opening afterward. We had a wonderful time and it seemed to me we made a pretty good team off screen as well as on. Neither of us was going with anyone special at the time, so we decided on each other. Our favorite night spot was Grace Hayes Lodge. We used to go there

Joy Hodges (third from left, standing), who helped Ronald Reagan get into films, joined veteran columnist Louella Parsons (seated) on her 1939 vaudeville tour that showcased other young Hollywood hopefuls, from left: Jane Wyman, Reagan, Arleen Whelan, unidentified man, June Preisser and Susan Hayward.

★ ★ ★

for dinner and sit and listen to our "theme song," "Deep Purple," and hold hands under the table.

A very romantic courtship? Yes, but the proposal was about as unromantic as any that ever happened. We were both working on a picture and were about to be called for a take. Ronnie simply turned to me as if the idea were brand new and had just hit him and said, "Jane, why don't we get married—?"

I couldn't think of any reason why we shouldn't. I'd been wondering for a whole year—ever since I first saw him—why he hadn't asked me. I was just about to say a definite yes when we were called before the cameras. In trying to step down off my own personal cloud, I managed to muff a few lines and toss in a whispered "Yes" after the director said, "Cut."

We were married January 26, at the Wee Kirk O'the Heather. It was a fairly small wedding, with Louella Parsons giving us a lovely reception afterward.

Jane Wyman
"How I Met My Husband"
by Jane Wyman and Alice Craig Greene
Motion Picture, August, 1946

★ ★ ★

First day back on the lot (after being in the service), Ronnie strolled in to say hello to the wardrobe boys, was snagged for a fitting. Pic'll be *Stallion Road*. Ronnie and b.w. Janie will co-star for the first time since wed in kitchen comedy *Out of the Frying Pan*, then he'll do movie of B'way hit *Voice of the Turtle*. Right now he's mainly interested in two things—the American Veterans Committee and horses! Ronnie's chairman of the Los Angeles AVC, recently authored anti-war resolution for chapter. He's determined this peace'll stick!

Movie Stars Parade
"Ronnie's Reconversion"
September, 1946

★ ★ ★

Janie and Ron Reagan are planning a new "Mr. and Mrs." screen series, will start after Ronnie finishes *Voice of the Turtle*.

Modern Screen
November, 1946

★ ★ ★

. . .Every family is different, I know. Perhaps the way in which my husband and I have arranged our lives couldn't be copied by others, but it *has* worked well, and *is* working well for us. Naturally, Ronnie and I married with the understanding that both of us were to go on with our careers. We wanted children, but that was to be an incident in the over-all development of our lives together, and was not viewed as a reason for my giving up the work in which I am quite as interested as Ronnie is.

. . .Ronnie and I have always arranged our picture schedules, whenever it was physically possible, so as to be at home with the children an hour before dinner, and they are

Brother Rat gave birth to a sequel, *Brother Rat and a Baby* (Warners, 1940), with the same principals (Wayne Morris, Priscilla Lane, Eddie Albert, Jane Bryan, Ronald Reagan and Jane Wyman) plus a new arrival (baby Peter B. Good).

★ ★ ★

allowed to remain up for an hour after dinner. When Michael was small, his feeding schedule was originally set in the afternoon at two, six and ten. The six o'clock feeding was inconvenient for Ronnie and me, so we simply re-arranged the schedule to read three, seven and eleven. In that way, Michael slept later in the morning, of course, so was able to romp with us when we came home from the studio.

Jane Wyman
"Career Mother," by Jane Wyman
Silver Screen, November, 1946

★ ★ ★

In Hollywood, Ronnie Reagan is regarded as an able young leader. From here on in, I think you will hear of Reagan in the national scene and of his wife, Jane Wyman, for everyone tells me they work as a team. Active member of the AVC, which is the most liberal of the veterans' organizations, Reagan is himself a liberal.

Adela Rogers St. Johns
"What the Hollywood Strikes Mean"
by Adela Rogers St. Johns
Photoplay, January, 1947

★ ★ ★

Each year Ronald Reagan sends Jane a nosegay of red and white roses with a card saying, "Happy Valentine's Day. . . From Me." This began the first Valentine's Day after they were married. Last year threatened to be a very unhappy one. When they got home from the studio the nosegay hadn't arrived. Which worried Reagan. And Janie, who had completely forgotten the date, was feeling unusually low. It had been one of those days when life piles everything up crosswise. "Good grief—what a day," she said tiredly, dropping into a chair. About that time a delivery truck drove up and the doorbell rang. "Now what?" she said, getting up to answer it. Ronnie grinned. Jane took the package and pulled out the familiar red and white bouquet. "Well—what do you know? It's Valentine's!" She looked at her husband affectionately and both started laughing. Jane bounced back to normal.

Maxine Arnold
"Be My Valentine," by Maxine Arnold
Photoplay, February, 1947

★ ★ ★

Not a doll, not a toy did young Maureen Reagan request, when Jane Wyman asked her daughter what she wanted for Christmas. "A picture of Claude Jarman, Jr.," said Miss Reagan, without hesitating. So Jane called up her "son" (in *The Yearling*) and had him autograph one. "At this rate," quipped Ronnie Reagan, when Jane related the incident

An Angel from Texas (Warners, 1940), was the third feature film appearance together of an eventual five for Reagan and Jane Wyman. It was also one of many screen versions of the George S. Kaufman play, *The Butter and Egg Man*.

that night at the dinner table, "when Maureen is ten, she'll probably want a date with Clark Gable!"

Weston East
"Here's Hollywood," by Weston East
Screenland, February, 1947

★ ★ ★

Jane Wyman proves she's a gal with a lot of sense as well as a lot of good looks. Because she has strict ideas about how her two kids are gonna be raised.

"For one thing," says Janie, "no interviews about 'em. It's a tough enough job for Holly-woodites to raise kids without their reading about themselves and getting an idea they're important."

Ronald Reagan agrees. And, although they'll let the photographers snap pictures of their little boy and girl, that's as far as the publicity goes.

Virginia MacPherson
"Let's Gossip," by Virginia MacPherson
Motion Picture, February, 1947

★ ★ ★

Millions of maudlin people ask them the same thing, so Jane and her Wild Irishman have the answer boiled down to a routine. Ronnie grins at her, she grins at him. "The secret of our happy life," they whoop, "is that (from Ronnie) we have (from Janie) MORE DARNED FUN!" (from both Reagans) and off they skip with a self-satisfied air. When they got married some six years ago, everybody thought it was practically an act of charity on Ronnie's part, marrying this mouse-brained cookie with the zany comedy sense and the jivey legs. Now she's up for an Oscar for playing Ma Baxter in *The Yearling* and the marriage mourners are wondering if Ronnie's role in *Stallion Road* will prevent his becoming known as Mr. Wyman. Silly people! Because to these kids, marriage is strictly silk against the flesh. Sure, Ronnie's near blind without his specs, but who says he can't enjoy those private movie showings with her after a lasagna splurge. And so what if she loves sambas and he dotes on Stokowski—get them together on a golf course and it's heaven below par.

Screen Album
1947

★ ★ ★

Jane Wyman and Ronald Reagan have arranged with their producers to leave their studio in time to dine at home at seven o'clock. They make an occasion of the dinner hour that is taken for granted in most families. Always Maureen, their six-year-old daughter, is at the table with them even though she has had supper earlier. First they hear about her day. Then Ronnie has the floor—until Jane says, "But you haven't heard a thing until you've heard my day!" Problems are taboo during this one time they all share.

Furthermore, Jane and Ronnie, both intensely interested in world affairs, have the same interests and the same friends. Ronnie does not have to get along as best he can with husbands of the women with whom Jane plays bridge and Jane does not have to wear a

A curtain call for the cast of *An Angel from Texas* (Warners, 1940). From left: Wayne Morris, Rosemary Lane, Eddie Albert, Jane Wyman and Ronald Reagan.

polite smile while the men Ronnie brings home to dinner talk business. In fact, Jane and Ronnie call each other on the phone two or three times a day to compare notes on the new ruling of the Screen Actors Guild or some rumor they've heard about television.

Elsa Maxwell
"Hollywood's Marriage Manners," by Elsa Maxwell
Photoplay, March, 1947

★ ★ ★

The Yearling premiere brought out all the stars in best bib and tucker. Dream walking was Janie Wyman in white lace and ermine escorted by proud hubby Ronnie Reagan. Ronnie turns director for series of WB sports shorts.

Movie Stars Parade
March, 1947

★ ★ ★

Question: What is your worst fault as a wife?
   Answer: Nagging Ron to clean out the garage. I don't let the poor man enjoy a day of leisure.

Jane Wyman
"Popping Questions at Jane Wyman"
by Helen Hover
Motion Picture, March, 1947

★ ★ ★

A Salute to Reagan. It seems to Cal that of all the people who have become motion picture actors, Ronald Reagan has taken firmer and more solid roots as a citizen who takes his responsibilities conscientiously and even weightily. He neither flinches nor falls down on duties that mean the advancement of what he believes to be right. In short, he is a sincere American who can be counted on one hundred per cent.

   Ronald hails from Dixon, Illinois, and as a typical American lad worked as lifeguard and radio sports announcer. We telephoned him recently with a message from the lovely Helen Altschuler, formerly of Dixon. He was instantly delighted, recalled how he had taught her daughter Sidney to swim and was pleased to hear that daughter was now a very pretty matron.

   It is this quality, we decided, plus his civic pride, that has made Reagan a respected and admired citizen. And while the career of his wife Jane Wyman has zoomed with *The Yearling*, his own has progressed with *Night unto Night* and *Stallion Road*. And for an unblemished marital record, we again salute a splendid gentleman!

Cal York
"Inside Stuff," by Cal York
Photoplay, May, 1947

★ ★ ★

Reagan's early breezy, even cocky screen image is well exemplified by this jaunty pose from *Murder in the Air* (Warners, 1940), in which he would play "Brass" Bancroft for the final time. "A" movies were coming up.

★ ★ ★

Wedding (of Ronald Reagan and Jane Wyman took place) at Wee Kirk O'the Heather Church. Third time for Jane, his first. Both were working in *Angel from Texas* at WB.

Movie Life
"Movie Life of Ronald Reagan"
June, 1947

★ ★ ★

"I have lived in the same house six years and still can't find the steps at night," she (Jane Wyman) said, laying dark glasses on the table. "I am farsighted."

"Ronnie can't see either," says Madame Reagan, who has no vanity.

Ronnie is nearsighted. It killed him because he couldn't get overseas with the cavalry, his wife says. He also suffered grave distress at the beach while tanning white circles away from his eyes. Chums would cry, "Pipe the shape hitting the waves!" Before Ronnie could locate his specs crying "Where, where?", the shape would vanish.

"He has got around that," says Mrs. Reagan. "He has found that by pulling up the corners of his eyes he can see well enough for the occasion. Squinting helps nearsighted people for a moment."

Herb Howe
"St. Joe's Jane," by Herb Howe
Photoplay, June, 1947

★ ★ ★

Hollywood newsreel:
    Ronald Reagan being mistaken for a clerk in a Hollywood department store.

Erskine Johnson
"Overheard in Hollywood," by Erskine Johnson
Motion Picture, June, 1947

★ ★ ★

Jane Wyman is lovelier than ever as she awaits arrival of the stork. Ronald Reagan looks at her adoringly as Art Weissman *(Screen Stars* Western Staff Photographer) captures the happiness of Hollywood's fabled "Perfect Couple."

The Observer
"Confidentially, The Gossip Corner"
by The Observer
Screen Stars, June, 1947

★ ★ ★

There's nothing coy about Wyman. She did the chasing, and doesn't give a hoot who knows it. When she and Ronnie met, he, too, was nursing a romantic scar, only his was fresher, and he thought he was through with girls.

One day, as she lunched at a table for two in The Green Room (at Warners) — this was after *Mr. Dodds Takes the Air* and before *Brother Rat* — in he walked. A voice halted him.

The turning point in Reagan's film career was the important supporting role of tragic football hero George (The Gipper) Gipp in *Knute Rockne, All American* (Warners, 1940). Star Pat O'Brien helped him get the part.

★ ★ ★

"Would you like to sit here?" She gave him the benefit of the big brown eyes.

He told her he'd seen *Mr. Dodds* in Des Moines, and liked her. Glenda Farrell came by. Glenda Farrell's a good egg. "We ran *Smart Blonde*, Janie. With you in the same studio, I'll have to watch my step."

Jane was feeling a little top-heavy, anyway. After all, she'd done thirty pictures to this character's two. "He must think I'm a great gal," she informed herself and went in search of a certain Mr. (Max) Arnow, talent chief at Warners.

"Look, you're always working on publicity for people. Sending them out to the nightspots together and so on. How about working it on this Reagan and me?"

"No. You ought to go out with a bigger name than your own. So should he."

Little girl, what now? Well, she was moving into her own apartment. Her beloved friend, Betsy Kaplan, was fixing it up for her. "When it's ready," said Betsy, "ask him over for cocktails."

Jane called him. "Let's have cocktails at my place."

"What for?"

Which stumped even Jane.

She knew when she was licked, and after that she laid her next campaign more cleverly. Ronnie spent most of his time with a bunch of his fraternity brothers. Swimming. Golfing. Riding. To Jane, the beach was a place where you got a suntan, but a girl can learn. She wormed her way into the graces of two fraternity brothers. All of a sudden she was a bug for outdoors. Ronnie started hearing what a swell scout the Wyman kid was. Before he knew it, she was one of them.

He proposed in a hospital room, after sending her roses with the loving message, RONALD REAGAN. Really sunk this time, Jane had shoved the roses off her bed and turned her face to the wall. That night Ronnie made the big discovery. All he wanted was to drive the sorrow out of her eyes. Suddenly, the world righted itself for them both.

Ida Zeitlin
"Jane Wyman Life Story," by Ida Zeitlin
Modern Screen, July, 1947

★ ★ ★

YOU. . .By Jane Wyman. You and I have been married seven years, Mr. Reagan. During this period, at least once a week you've reminded me (kiddingly) how lucky I am to have you for a husband. I think I *am* lucky.

You love to tell stories at my expense, especially that one about our first meeting ten years ago, when we were making *Brother Rat*. According to you, I took one good look and said to myself, "Janie, this is *it*." Well, that's just the way it *did* happen.

You know, I don't think I have ever seen you *really* angry—but I'd hate to cause you to lose your temper. There was that one time: I was wrong and we both knew it. You believe there is a reason for everything, so as usual, you were tolerant and took an objective viewpoint. I think your understanding is your greatest of many sweet qualities. Don't get the idea that I think you're a perfect husband, however. If you were, I'd be bored to death.

Remember when you rushed home and explained: "Janie, I want to take you someplace. Now don't ask any questions, just come along." I kept trying to guess whether it was going to be an emerald or a new mink!

We finally stopped in front of a funny, little old building. You leaped out of the car and opened the door like a knight. It's the *new* Ronald Reagan, I kept telling myself. To you I said: "Why in the world are you bringing me here? What do they have inside?" "Turtle

Wyman and Reagan in one of the less turbulent moments from *Tugboat Annie Sails Again* (Warners, 1940). The popularity of both players was rising, and so were their temperatures: they were married on January 26, 1940.

food," you shouted enthusiastically, "I'm going to start an aquarium and, Janie, they have the finest turtle food in town!" "That's great," I answered grimly. "Now the world can relax."

But all kidding aside, there isn't a single thing about you I'd want to change. You've been wonderful for me in many ways. You know how easily I blow up and have to get things off my chest. You're just the opposite, and it has a soothing effect. Actually, you are a serious person, but you use a humorous approach. It's a great gift, Ronnie. Calmly and quietly, with that keen analytical mind, you get the most amazing results.

And now you're pretty thrilled that once again we're stalking the stork. They tell me you told the gang on Warners' *Voice of the Turtle* that you hope we can name her Veronica. Personally, I prefer Ronald, Jr., and this I want you to know. Regardless, it will still be "Ronnie" to me.

Your love of sports has given you a clean mind, to say nothing of a clean body. How well I know! Two baths and two bath towels a day. Remind me to tell you a bedtime story about the laundry situation. Your room is always neat, everything you own in immaculate order. You never even put away a pair of shoes without first buffing them. You're a sentimentalist: you remember holidays; you've never forgotten an anniversary. On these occasions you buy me presents, and a card always comes with them. I love these cards and I save them. They're witty and tender. You write as well as you act—and jump horses.

If you promise to do something you never go back on your word. On the other hand, you're a past master at postponing (in case you didn't notice it—I hired a man to move the dog house and clean out the garage). You try to hide what you're thinking when I indulge in my favorite indoor sport of re-arranging the furniture. I guess the only thing we heartily disagree on is dancing—together. We get along so beautifully with other partners but I suspect that I unconsciously do the leading. You never say anything.

Jane Wyman
Movies, August, 1947

★ ★ ★

There was nothing revolutionary (with one possible exception) about the particular scene they were shooting for *The Voice of the Turtle*. The sound stage was churning—make-up men, hairdressers, wardrobe women—the usual people automatically performing their usual duties. Clutter, chatter, utter confusion that magically dissolves itself into coordination the second they start rolling.

In the center of the set there was a bed. A good-looking young man was lying there quietly, peacefully, relaxed. His eyes were closed, the corners of his mouth curved in a slight smile. Persistent prop men pushed the bed first to the left, then to the right. Electricians adjusted huge swaying lamps that groaned and shuddered, as heavy black cables impeded their progress. Completely oblivious, the prone passenger, Ronald Reagan, continued to lay there—*fast asleep!*

Finally they were ready to shoot. Eleanor Parker in the role made famous by Margaret Sullavan in the theater was called into the scene. Wearing new thick bangs that made her pert and prettier (if possible), she took her place at Ronnie's bedside. Director Irving Rapper walked over, put his hand on the slumberer's shoulders and gently shook him.

"Wake up, Ronnie," he kidded. "You are supposed to be *acting* on Mr. Warner's time!"

Ronnie stretched, yawned, displayed no embarrassment.

"Acting, he says," Ronnie went along with the gag. "I'm *supposed* to be asleep in this scene. I give you the *real* thing—an Academy Award performance! The way I look at it,

Reagan, Olivia de Havilland and Errol Flynn in *The Santa Fe Trail* (Warners, 1940).
According to Reagan, Flynn—insecure despite his magnetism—often tried to usurp Reagan's
best scenes for himself.

Mr. Warner's making money on the deal. Besides, I left Janie and the kids at Palm Springs at five o'clock this morning and drove all the way back. I'm three hours behind in the shut-eye department."

It couldn't possibly have happened before—before those four years in the service, to be exact. It's a changed Ronnie Reagan. . .(Before), he was still too intense at times, prone to take his work so seriously that he got very little kick out of it in return.

Jerry Asher
"The Reformation of Ronnie," by Jerry Asher
Screenland, September, 1947

★ ★ ★

Recently, Ronnie was asked if he'd like to run for Senator. He appreciated the honor but he declined it gracefully. "I'm a happy man just the way things are," he answered. "And I believe in letting well enough alone."

Screenland
September, 1947

★ ★ ★

Ann Sheridan and Jane Wyman, longtime friends, were exchanging "remember whens." "I'll never forget," said Ann, "the wild ride Ronnie (Ronald Reagan) gave me for that scene in *Juke Girl*. I felt as though the car was going full speed ahead with no one at the wheel."

"So did I," recalled Jane. "After all, Ronnie didn't have his glasses on and I knew he couldn't see the radiator cap, much less the road."

Erskine Johnson
"Overheard in Hollywood," by Erskine Johnson
Motion Picture, October, 1947

★ ★ ★

Although Viveca Lindfors' Swedish accent is still quite noticeable, other members of the cast (of *Night unto Night*) were amazed that she spoke English as well as she did. That was because she studied English in school, then had a rigorous brushing-up course two months before coming to this country. Two of the cast's pranksters, Ronald Reagan and Broderick Crawford, spent hours teaching her new slang, much of it unprintable. Then they would wait patiently, for hours if necessary, to hear their pupil blurt out her new and ofttimes startling linguistic accomplishments. She took it all good-naturedly, but often threatened Reagan and Crawford with drastic revenge if she should ever get them in a Swedish film.

Movie Story
"On the Set of *Night unto Night*"
November, 1947

★ ★ ★

Newlyweds Jane Wyman and Ronald Reagan at breakfast in 1940.

★ ★ ★

Ronald Reagan admits to a quick, hot, door-slamming temper that wears off in less than a day.

Cal York
"Inside Stuff," by Cal York
Photoplay, December, 1947

★ ★ ★

It was just before Christmas in New York. Jane Wyman paced the length and breadth of her hotel suite, awaiting a call from La Guardia Airport.

The telephone rang. An official voice said, "Sorry, Mrs. Reagan, planes still grounded—ceiling zero."

Jane's voice was urgent. "I'll stand by. Keep calling."

Her pacing was resumed together with her vigils at the windows that framed a city blanketed in fog. Back and forth went little Miss Button-nose (so pet-named by her husband) awaiting the wanted word from La Guardia that she could plane back to Holly-wood—*back to Ronnie?*

Yet only the night before, Jane had told a friend, "We're finished, and it's all my fault."

Three times before, Jane had said goodbye to her marriage, then reconciled.

Is this the last round in the marriage ring that has encircled the fighting Reagans for ten sometimes stormy but all the time, we believe, in-love years?

That Ronnie is still deeply in love with Jane is very evident. In fact, he says so. When reached in Hollywood, and faced with Jane's latest verdict on their marriage, Ronnie announced with a wry but unmistakably tender smile, "It's a strange character I'm married to. But I love her."

That Jane is still deeply in love with Ronnie (or why her frantic eagerness to get back to where he was?) is, in our opinion, also very evident. "We're finished," she says. But somehow we do not take this too seriously. Words can be so many little masks to cover up the heart.

"They were blissfully happy together," a close friend says of them, "until the war came"...

Gladys Hall
"Those Fightin' Reagans," by Gladys Hall
Photoplay, February, 1948

★ ★ ★

"If this comes to a divorce," sighed Ronnie, with bitter humor, "I think I'll name *Johnny Belinda* co-respondent!"

Johnny Belinda is the picture Jane finished just before she disappeared from Hollywood "for a rest." *Johnny Belinda*. Well, you might as well give the villain a name in the oldest, saddest story there is to tell in Hollywood (and one I never thought I'd be telling about Jane Wyman and Ronald Reagan). The plot's a triangle, and you can call that sinister third party Career or Ambition or whatever you like. But *Johnny Belinda* will do.

I can't really believe it yet. I talked to Ronnie the day he read Jane's statement in the newspapers. That was the day Jane, driven to the point of collapse by too much work, too much forcing herself along the path of ambition, lost her battle and lost her head, and told an inquiring reporter that her marriage happiness had to pay the bill.

Reagan was loaned to posh MGM Studios to appear with Laraine Day and Wallace Beery in *The Bad Man* (1941), from a vintage, previously filmed Western play.

That day Ronnie talked to me in puzzled voice (he'd just come home from a Christmas shopping trip, after buying presents for his wife and their darlings, Maureen and Michael).

"I love Jane, and I know she loves me," he said. "I don't know what this is all about, and I don't know why Jane has done it. For my part I hope to live with her for the rest of my life."

I always thought Jane and Ronnie Reagan were one of the best-balanced, merriest, feet-on-the-ground couples around town. There are some differences in their temperament, of course. Ronnie's easygoing; Jane's high-strung. But only lately have these things mattered.

. . .Last June, Jane's baby was born, three months too soon. She didn't live.

Jane should never have started work on any picture as soon as she did after her family tragedy. In *Johnny Belinda*, Jane tackled a job that would test a Bernhardt. She plays a deaf mute in a highly emotional role. . .Jane lost twenty pounds. She started plump from her motherhood. By the time she wobbled off the last scene, she looked like a ghost, her eyes large in their sockets.

. . .Ronnie, being the sweet guy that he is, understood and tried to help. He coaxed her out, whenever he could, to dine and dance her nerves away. But it didn't work. She couldn't forget herself or her part for a minute. She was sullen, rude and jittery, even to Ronnie. She couldn't touch a relaxing cocktail without letting it go to her head. Usually Ronnie took her home early.

One night, outside the Beverly Club, Jane blew a fuse. As Ronnie helped her into the car, she was talking loudly and angrily. "I've got along without you before," she cried, "and I certainly can get along without you now!" Onlookers who overheard shrugged it off. "A spat."

But there weren't many storm warnings like that. Not until the very last day of *Johnny Belinda*, when the pressure was finally off. There was a little cast-and-crew party after the last take, and Jane announced that she was taking a rest. "With Ronnie and the kids?" somebody asked.

"No," Jane said wearily. "Just me."

. . .If Ronald Reagan is responsible in any way for this threat to his happiness and the happiness of the girl he loves, I'd say it's because he has been too nice, too sympathetic with Jane, too good-naturedly content to let her run herself ragged.

Hedda Hopper
"A Good Man is Hard to Find," by Hedda Hopper
Modern Screen, March, 1948

★   ★   ★

The trial separation of Jane Wyman and Ronald Reagan was another surprise. Hollywood was really banking on this marriage to last. My prediction is that they will patch up their differences, if they haven't already done so by the time you read this.

Erskine Johnson
"Overheard in Hollywood," by Erskine Johnson
Motion Picture, March, 1948

★   ★   ★

I can take movie stars or leave them alone, and movie stars have always reciprocated in kind. But the Reagans—they were different; they were my friends. We used to swap pic-

The role of a pianist was another step up the ladder for Ronald Reagan (left) in *Milion Dollar Baby* (Warners, 1941), co-starring with Priscilla Lane and Jeffrey Lynn.

★ ★ ★

tures of our kids, we used to stay at each other's houses — to me, the Reagans symbolized all that was pleasant and honest in Hollywood. Now that they've split up, I feel I've lost something. Because the Reagans were pets of *Modern Screen* readers. You loved them; you adopted them; you're going to miss them. I know.

Jane and Ronnie were already separated when I made my last trip to Hollywood. . .I went back in my mind to the beginning. . .

Birthdays, Christmases — you shared them all with the Reagans. Christmas of '43, when it was hard to get ornaments (because of the war), and the tree looked skimpy, partly because the star for the top had been used to trim a tiny tree in Maureen's room, and Maureen coming into the living room Christmas morning, and walking quietly over to the big tree, and saying sadly, "Poor tree. Yere's no star on top."

Yes, we shared the good times and the bad times with Ronnie and Jane, and finally the war was over, and Ronnie was home, and it should have been all-clear from there. But who's got a crystal ball? If you'd asked me, for instance, a little while back, I'd have said this was one of the best years in Jane's life. She got some real career breaks. The role in *Lost Weekend*. Ma Baxter in *The Yearling*. But Ma Baxter got her the Academy nomination, and people who like to talk about trouble say that's when the trouble started.

. . .Still the talk went on. "Jane lost her baby girl last June — that's what made her neurotic." And: "Jane should see a psychiatrist." Everybody getting into the act.

Jane'll have custody of the children. "I believe children are better off with their mother," Ronnie said, "and Jane's a wonderful mother. I'll have the privilege of seeing them."

The statement gives me a lump in my throat. I guess there's nothing more to say. When a beautiful dream is over, you wake up reluctantly; you face the real, harsh world. If the Reagans are through, I'm sorry. They meant a lot to me.

Albert P. Delacorte
"Unhappy Ending," by Albert P. Delacorte
Modern Screen, 1948

Maureen Reagan, 6-year-old daughter of the Ronald Reagans, made her debut as a dancer in the presentation of *The Nutcracker Suite* by the Ballet Russe in Los Angeles. She captivated the entire cast and the audience with her performance — also by the fact that while everyone else performed, she sat back and yawned. Then, not having been tipped off, she joined the ballerina in all the bows — after which she walked off the stage into her dad's arms, and fell promptly asleep.

Carl Schroeder
"Behind the Scenes with Carl Schroeder"
Motion Picture, March, 1948

As this is written, Ronald Reagan and Jane Wyman are still separated, but it is to be hoped that a reconciliation soon takes place. Hollywood sympathy in this case is one hundred per cent with Ronnie, who is a prince. Jane is a moody person, temperamental, ambitious, restless and seeking; furthermore, she is not now and hasn't been well for some time. It is

Reagan made four films with Warners' popular ingenue Priscilla Lane (right), including *Million Dollar Baby* (1941). Also prominent was beloved veteran actress May Robson, who died the following year.

to be hoped that, as her health improves, Jane's other problems will vanish, and two of the town's favorite people will resume their marriage.

Fredda Dudley
"Hollywood Earfuls," by Fredda Dudley
Silver Screen, April, 1948

★　★　★

When the feudin' and fussin' between Ronald and Jane Wyman turned out to be serious, after all, Warners hastily changed plans to co-star them in *John Loves Mary*—and brought Patricia Neal out from Broadway for the role opposite Ronnie. She's so pretty that, to keep the wolf pack at bay (at least until the finish of the picture), Ronnie is personally escorting her to the night spots.

Movie Story
"Movie Story's Gossip," April, 1948

★　★　★

It is unfortunate but true, that Hollywood can shrug off most marriage crack-ups. . .

But when they are Jane Wyman and Ronald Reagan—well—we just can't take that!

No marital separation since I broke the story that Mary Pickford, America's sweetheart, was leaving Douglas Fairbanks, has had the effect of the parting of the Reagans. Just as Mary and Doug stood for all that is best in this town, so have Ronnie and Jane. They seemed so thoroughly congenial, were such model parents who, as citizens, recognized their duty to their community and their profession.

For eight years they have shared a beautiful life that has earned them the respect and admiration even of people who did not know them personally. To those of us who are close friends, they were an ideal Mr. and Mrs.

That's why this hurts so much. That's why we are fighting so hard to make them realize that what seems to have come between them is not important enough to make their break final. I know this is what Ronnie, himself, hopes will happen.

But perhaps we are fighting too hard. Jane said to me, not so long ago: *"If people would only let us alone!* If our friends would only stop trying to run our lives, maybe we would have a chance to regain happiness."

. . .At the time of their break I had asked Jane if she thought Ronnie's duties as president of the Screen Actors Guild had taken too much of his time. She said, "Of course not. Ronnie is magnificent in this big job and I'm very proud of him."

Louella O. Parsons
"Last Call for Happiness," by Louella O. Parsons
Photoplay, April, 1948

★　★　★

Reagan received top billing in an "A" film for the first time in *International Squadron* (Warners, 1941), with Olympe Bradna as the female lead. It was a remake of Cagney's *Ceiling Zero*.

Eleanor Parker is blonde, green-eyed and so beautiful that Ronald Reagan, who plays opposite her in *The Voice of the Turtle*, admits that kissing her is a breath-taking experience.

Photoplay
"Parker's Progress," April, 1948

★ ★ ★

People on the Warner Brothers lot won't easily forget how Sweden's Viveca Lindfors "made back with the jokes" during her first picture here. All through *Night unto Night* Ronnie Reagan, Viveca's co-star, made sly references to dates, to a rendezvous or two. "Look, Svenska," Reagan would whisper, "Janie's away in New York. (This, of course, was long before any talk of divorce.) We can go places, have fun. You know." Viveca would listen quietly, her blue eyes humorous and a little speculative. Others in the cast played up to Reagan's ribbing. To top off the gag, the unit publicity girl on the picture pretended she had "planted" the story of the Lindfors–Reagan "romance" with the Associated Press as a piece of hot news. "So?" said Viveca. "I see."

That afternoon a couple of top Hollywood columnists were on the set, chatting with Miss Lindfors, when the unsuspecting Reagan walked in. "Ronnie! My darling!" cried Viveca, rushing up to him and flinging her arms around him. "Oh, I am so happy you have come back to me." (She had left him only a half hour before, when Reagan had gone out for a Coke and a hamburger.) Before the startled Reagan knew what was happening Viveca had kissed him—a long, lingering, passionate kiss.

"Hey, what gives here?" cried Ronnie.

"But, darling," said Viveca, too innocently, "we are in love, no?" She looked about her, at the grinning columnists and the now red-faced publicity girl. "You give the newspapers a story about us; you say we are in love. It should not be—how you say?—a phony, no?"

That neat bit of table-turning took care of the ribbing. For a while, anyway.

Favius Friedman
"Swedish Modern," by Favius Friedman
Motion Picture, July, 1948

★ ★ ★

It was the night of Joan Crawford's party for Noel Coward, with all of Hollywood's elite invited. Everyone was having a wonderful time—except for one guest.

Jane Wyman came into the room alone, looked around at the happy throng, then burst into tears. Shortly afterward she left.

Before her reconciliation with Ronald Reagan late in April, Jane had been behaving as though she were on the verge of a nervous breakdown. She had gone into tantrums in public, burst into tears on slight provocation, given hysterical statements to reporters. "I'm going to divorce Ronnie. . .No, we're going to reconcile. . .The reconciliation didn't work. . .There's going to be a trial separation. . .It's all over. . ."

If the Reagans had not for so long been so obviously happy together, and if Jane had not been behaving so much like a woman torn by inner conflicts she couldn't seem to solve, all this might have passed off as just another incident in Hollywood's long record of unhappy marriages.

But Jane wasn't behaving like a girl who had calmly thought things through. She gave

Faye Emerson, who would marry President Roosevelt's son Elliott, performed with the future President of the United States, Ronald Reagan, in the "B" movie *Nine Lives Are Not Enough* (Warners, 1941). Also shown: Edward Brophy and James Gleason.

★ ★ ★

every sign of being physically and emotionally strained. Even though she and Ronnie have now reconciled, the important question is still: What's ahead for Jane Wyman?

Laura Pomeroy
"What's Ahead for Jane Wyman?", by Laura Pomeroy
Motion Picture, July, 1948

★ ★ ★

A reconciliation that didn't take was that of Jane Wyman and Ronald Reagan. She has moved out again to a house at Mailbu Beach and has filed for divorce. Her new interest in life is said to be Manny Sachs.

Movie Story
"Movie Story's Gossip"
August, 1948

★ ★ ★

Ronald Reagan and Jane Wyman were all ready to patch up their troubles when Jane served Ronald with divorce papers. Friends say the bloom faded off the rose when Ronnie began taking her too much for granted and spent all his spare time in his shop where he goes in for brass work. His great occupation with politics, Screen Actors Guild affairs and world problems also irked her. Warners studio bosses had even given the actor time off by delaying his next picture so the couple could take a second honeymoon. At this writing Ronnie is still trying to get Jane to change her mind about the divorce.

Screen Guide
August, 1948

★ ★ ★

Jane Wyman believes in saying it with a car and delivering it, even when the romance is over. A few months before she gave Ronald Reagan his marching papers Jane ordered a 1948 swank car as a big surprise for him. It certainly was. Because it arrived at his front door, tied with a big blue bow, the week *after* he moved out of the house he used to share with Jane and the children. He kept the car, of course—new cars are hard to get!

Sheilah Graham
"They Say It with Presents," by Sheilah Graham
Photoplay, October, 1948

★ ★ ★

About two years ago, Jane Wyman and Ronald Reagan stood outside their hilltop home and talked about the new house they planned to build.

Suddenly Jane's eyes grew moist. "You know, Ronnie," she said, "I hate to leave this house. Of course, it's gotten too small for us, but it's meant so much to us."

It was the first home they'd bought. Ronnie had designed the floor plans. . .and Jane had decorated it. . .

Kings Row (Warners, 1942), is Reagan's favorite among his pictures. He portrayed amputee Drake McHugh in the film version of Henry Bellamann's novel of seamy small-town doings. Above, Robert Cummings, Ann Sheridan and Reagan.

★ ★ ★

Now the house is up for sale. . .Jane has turned her back on the house and all those memories, and plans to live in Malibu Beach this summer with their two children. . .

With apartments so hard to find (even for movie stars) he called their former apartment house manager and asked if there was a vacancy. Yes, there was one — and as fate would have it, the very one he and Jane had lived in so happily once upon a time! And there Ronnie is living now, with the ghosts of honeymoon memories surrounding him.

. . .Whenever there's a divorce in Hollywood, suspicious Hollywood looks around for the "other man" and the "other woman." In this case, there is truthfully no other man or woman. Since Jane separated from Ronnie, she has been seen frequently with Manny Sachs, a recording company executive.

Jane says, her eyes snapping, "Why shouldn't I see Manny? He used to be my agent, and Ronnie and I have known him for years. How can anybody call that a romance?"

As for Ronnie, even cynical Hollywood has never coupled his name with that of another woman.

So why should two people who for eight years were a symbol of Hollywood's happiest couples come to the point where they decided to break?

The answer is to be found in two temperaments that were never really right for each other.

Elizabeth Shelley
"Finis," by Elizabeth Shelley
Movieland, September, 1948

★ ★ ★

Why I've refused to talk to certain reporters:

It certainly is no secret that I am now divorced from Ronald Reagan. There are two people who know the causes and the reasons — Ronnie and myself. We have never discussed them for publication. We never will. We consider it our own personal business. *Many* "inside" stories have been written about our breakup, all of them unauthentic and unauthorized. Writers and reporters play an important part in helping all of us get established. I've made many friends who've respected my wishes in refusing to discuss my problems. Unfortunately, there are those who have probed and prodded, so naturally I have avoided them.

Jane Wyman
"Why I've Changed," by Jane Wyman
Photoplay, October, 1948

★ ★ ★

Most lamented divorce was that of Jane Wyman and Ronald Reagan, who had seemed one of Hollywood's solidest couples. It's said that Jane entered so wholeheartedly into her role as a deaf-mute in Warners' *Johnny Belinda* that she lived it at home, too. However, two have been seen lunching together — and the divorce isn't final yet!

Movie Life
January, 1949

★ ★ ★

Reagan's stock soared after *Kings Row* (Warners, 1942), with Ann Sheridan again his leading lady. The picture was a great popular hit and afforded Reagan one of his meatiest roles.

★ ★ ★

Maybe the Ronald Reagan–Jane Wyman marriage will be back in good standing by the time you read this. Their differences were minor, actually, and since they've been separated, neither one has found a vital interest in anyone of the opposite sex. I happen to know that they've been seeing a lot more of each other than people know about. They've talked over their problems, taken another look at the kids — and I'd say, just about decided to start housekeeping again. Maybe if they made a picture together they'd fall right back into the companionable groove they once occupied. Okay, Warner Brothers, take it from there.

Movie Stars Parade
February, 1949

★ ★ ★

There was plenty of excitement at Slapsie Maxie's when Jane and her escort, Manny Sachs, were seated at the table next to Ronnie Reagan and Ann Sothern. But the other ringsiders who were watching to see Ronnie and Jane cold-shoulder each other were disappointed on account of they all chatted very amiably.

Screenland
February, 1949

★ ★ ★

It has been granted that the difference between her (Jane Wyman's) career and Ronnie's had a great deal to do with their initial breach. No girl can possibly be a fine actress without being fascinated by her own portrayals, and no man can watch his wife become important without trying to save his face. Ronnie did the perfectly natural thing. He became immersed in outside activities. The Guild, politics, even his old college held his attention more and more. Eventually the Reagans were left with very little in common to discuss except their expected baby.

But that was almost enough. They both wanted the new baby with all their hearts. Jane, however, had a tough pregnancy, and the final blow was the baby's death immediately after its premature birth.

Ruth Waterbury
"This is a Love Story," by Ruth Waterbury
Photoplay, March, 1949

★ ★ ★

The award Jane Wyman received as best actress of the year from the *London Daily Express* Film Tribunal was accepted in London by none other than her ex, Ronald Reagan, who was in England at the time making *The Hasty Heart*.

Ronnie's and Jane's young son, Michael, was in the bad graces of his mother when he at-

Distinguished set designer William Cameron Menzies was a major reason for the success of *Kings Row* (Warners, 1942), starring Ann Sheridan and Ronald Reagan. Pair is pictured above emoting against one of Menzies' rural sound stage creations.

tempted to improve on one of her landscape paintings by daubing it generously with a tube of gold paint.

Lynn Bowers
"What Hollywood Itself is Talking About!"
by Lynn Bowers
Screenland, May, 1949

★ ★ ★

A few weeks before (she won the 1948 Academy Award for *Johnny Belinda*), I'd seen Jane Wyman and Lew Ayres together at the Errol Flynn party. Jane looked happier than I'd seen her for a long time. Lew, his thin, tanned face responsive to her every remark, looked happy, too. They spent most of the evening chatting with the Ronald Colmans. Every once in a while, Jane would wander off to greet her friends, and Lew would remain where he was, waiting for her. . .

Watching them together, I thought back to *Johnny Belinda* and the tender love scenes these two played in it at the time Jane was getting ready to call quits to her marriage.

I don't believe for a minute that Lew, or any other man, was responsible for the break in what Hollywood had long considered the "perfect marriage." I'm sure that Jane had decided quite a while before she and Lew made *Johnny Belinda* that she and Ronnie Reagan were heading in different directions. However, when a girl is already emotionally at odds with her husband, close association with another man, attractive and considerate, might cause her to view her mate with an even more critical eye.

. . .As I watched them at Errol's party, they were having lots of laughs and both seemed very intent on what the other was saying.

This scene contrasted so sharply with one I'd witnessed when I watched Jane and Ronnie dining at Le Papillon on The Strip, just before she took off for New York where she finally admitted she was separating from her husband. They weren't laughing at all, and their few smiles were pretty wooden. Once or twice Ronnie went into long dissertations, and I gathered from Jane's expression that she was pretty uninterested in what he was saying.

Janet Franklin
"Winner Take All?!", by Janet Franklin
Modern Screen, June, 1949

★ ★ ★

Ronald Reagan, film actor, received a multiple fracture of the right thigh in a baseball game between leading men and comedians at Wrigley Field, Dr. Daniel H. Levinthal announced yesterday.

When Reagan was hurt in a slide to first base it was first thought that he had strained a ligament. He was taken to the Santa Monica Hospital and placed in a traction cast. He is expected to be a hospital patient for between six and eight weeks.

Los Angeles Daily News
June 21, 1949

★ ★ ★

Lieut. Ronald Reagan, holding first-born infant daughter Maureen Elizabeth, says "So long, Button Nose" to first wife Jane Wyman as he leaves for the Army in April, 1942.

★ ★ ★

Back from his four-months' stay in England, where he starred in *The Hasty Heart*, Ronald Reagan wants to gain weight and get a suntan.

Modern Screen
July, 1949

★ ★ ★

Jane Wyman, Academy Award winner, has her final divorce papers from Ronald Reagan.

Miss Wyman, 33, obtained the decree yesterday. When granted an interlocutory decree last year, she testified that Reagan, 37, was too absorbed in politics as president of the Screen Actors Guild.

A settlement gave her custody of their two children, $500 monthly for their support and an equal division of $75,000 worth of community property.

Hollywood Citizen–News
July 19, 1949

★ ★ ★

Before starting another picture commitment, Ann Sheridan quietly checked into the St. John's Hospital. Frankly, her friends are worried. Ever since she contracted pneumonia in Europe, Annie hasn't been able to lose that hacking cough. She's lost a lot of weight, too, but her doctor says nothing serious is wrong. While she was waiting for his verdict, Ann and Ronnie Reagan exchanged jokes, via the telephone. He was convalescing on the floor below from that broken leg.

Donald McClure
"Hollywood Earfuls," by Donald McClure
Silver Screen, November, 1949

★ ★ ★

A reconciliation for the Ronald Reagans? With all our heart we wish that were the reason why he moved into Jane Wyman's house. But it doesn't work that way. Janie was still in London making *Stage Fright*. When Ronnie quit the hospital, she suggested he go to her house to be near their children. Also, her servants could prepare his meals while he learned to get around on crutches. Hollywood should be proud of the intelligent way these two have handled their personal problems.

Frances Franklin
"Topics for Gossip," by Frances Franklin
Silver Screen, November, 1949

★ ★ ★

Ronald Reagan's out of the hospital, but that broken leg will keep him on crutches until Christmas. Despite those eight tortured weeks in traction, there were still compensations. Amongst his daily visitors were Ann Sothern, Patricia Neal, Ruth Roman and Shirley Ballard. Ronnie had other entertainment, too. "I watched television morning, noon and

Jane Wyman and Ronald Reagan attend the Hollywood premiere of the film *Yankee Doodle Dandy* (Warners, 1942), for which star James Cagney won that year's best actor Academy Award.

★ ★ ★

night," he grins. "In fact, I saw so many old Westerns, when I quit the hospital I was calling the nurses 'Mam' and speaking with a slow drawl!"

Silver Screen
November, 1949

★ ★ ★

He was recently divorced from Jane Wyman, and in the Hollywood fashion, they remain friends. They have two children, Maureen Elizabeth, age 9, and Michael Edward, 5. Jane has a painting of him in her dressing room. He often visits and watches her when she is working. She doesn't visit him on his set.

He has been going with Nancy Davis, a pretty model. He has also been linked with Monica Lewis, Adele Jergens and Patricia Neal. They are all just dates. He also takes out Jane Wyman. His idea of a date is to take Nancy, Monica or Pat to a restaurant for dinner. This takes hours, for he talks and talks. Occasionally he likes to go dancing.

Sidney Skolsky
Hollywood Citizen-News
December 8, 1949

★ ★ ★

Reagan and Sheridan were announced originally to star in *Casablanca*, but instead they drew *Juke Girl* (Warners, 1942) while Bogart and Bergman went on to *Casablanca*—and screen immortality. Also shown above: at left, Howard da Silva; at right, Ray Teal.

The 1950S

The Treasury Department. . . shows that in 1946 Humphrey Bogart received $432,000; Bette Davis $328,000; Bing Crosby $325,000; Deanna Durbin $325,477; Betty Grable $299,333; Ann Sheridan $269,345; Robert Montgomery $250,000; Errol Flynn $199,999; Rosalind Russell $190,104; Ronald Reagan $169,750; Rita Hayworth $94,916.

Hortense Powdermaker
Hollywood: The Dream Factory
by Hortense Powdermaker
Little, Brown Publishers, 1950

★ ★ ★

When Jane Wyman returned from England, Ronald Reagan was in New York on Screen Actors Guild business. She didn't even know they were in the same hotel until he called her. They talked, but didn't get together.

Silver Screen
January, 1950

★ ★ ★

Six hundred Friars and their fraus gathered last night at the Beverly Hills Hotel in honor of Ronald Reagan. Though everyone present had different reasons for being on hand to honor the Screen Actors Guild prexy, all reasons were good.

   With the ladies — the reasons ranged from fact he was a good actor to fact he was handsome. With the men, the reasons were slightly different — his stature and dignity in the industry, his understanding and sincere regard for his fellow man, his fairness and kindness in all dealings; one of Hollywood's most popular men was being honored because Hollywood and the industry love him.

   This was not a roast. It was anything but.

Daily Variety
February 9, 1950

★ ★ ★

We asked Ruth Roman about her romance with Ronald Reagan, and she said that the romance amounted to three dates — that was all — and she didn't know the fellow well enough to be getting serious.

   Incidentally, Ronnie is getting mighty fed up on those swell guy roles he's been getting since the war. He wants to play a meanie for a change.

Reagan portrayed a yank in the RAF in *Desperate Journey* (Warners, 1942). Above, from left: Reagan, Nancy Coleman, Errol Flynn (who got top billing) and Arthur Kennedy.

★ ★ ★

Ronnie gave his ex-wife, Jane Wyman, a toy French poodle, which is almost her constant companion. She even carries it to the studio in her blouse.

Movieland
"Inside Hollywood"
April, 1950

★　★　★

When I signed with Warner Brothers, my first picture assignment of importance was the lead in *The Girl from Jones Beach*, opposite Ronald Reagan. I had heard a great deal of praise for Ronnie, but in my opinion no one has ever quite told the full story of his sweetness and generosity.

I should explain one thing before telling about working with Ronnie: the general public seems to believe that an actress is a girl entirely without humility or self-doubt. Such a conception of almost any actress is mistaken. . .The idea of having to spend much time before the camera in a bathing suit bothered me. It's true that I have worn dozens of abbreviated costumes of various types, but a bathing suit is the most unfriendly of outfits. It can't keep a secret.

The day I walked out of my dressing room, wearing one of the daring white swim suits required for the part, I expected my knees to bang together and my teeth to click.

Then a wonderful thing happened. Ronnie Reagan, who has the manners of a grand duke under ordinary circumstances, WHISTLED at me. That wolf call did more for my ego and my self-assurance than a hundred words could have done.

Ronnie gave me confidence in other ways. Without making a point of the fact that I was a newcomer on the lot—hence strange to traditional practices—he put me wise to a good many things. Also, whenever any one of the dozens of department heads or studio officials came on the set, Ronnie managed to be near me and to point out important people, giving me the correct names and titles, before I was officially introduced. Anyone who has ever been the new employee in a large corporation will understand my gratitude to Ronnie. He guided me about the difficult ways of doing a good public relations job, and helped me to gain confidence in my ability to meet people—all kinds of people from messenger boys to millionaires.

Virginia Mayo
"Men Have Given Me Confidence," by Virginia Mayo
Movieland, April, 1950

★　★　★

Dinner Data: Ronald Reagan, facing the dais, not four feet from his ex-wife, Jane Wyman, smiled more broadly, clapped louder than any other person in the audience when she received the *Photoplay* Gold Medal for her performance in *Johnny Belinda*. Just a few nights before, Jane in the same room (the Crystal Room of the Beverly Hills Hotel) attended a Friars Frolic during which Ronnie received accolades from that organization. It was Jane, then, who paid beaming tribute to her ex-husband. So many in town are still hoping that these two will reconcile.

Photoplay
May, 1950

★　★　★

Anti-Nazi derring-do was the focus of *Desperate Journey* (Warners, 1942), with (above, from left) Alan Hale, Reagan, Errol Flynn and Arthur Kennedy.

When Universal-International hosted a "family premiere" at the Carthay Circle Theatre, all the stars and press turned out with their relatives. Ann Blyth arrived with her aunt and uncle, Ronald Reagan escorted his mother, ditto Scott Brady, Piper Laurie and Anthony Curtis. Jane Wyman also attended the showing (ex-hubby Reagan stars in the movie, *Louisa*), but came alone. Clever invitations announced: "Bundling by the grandparents, sparking by the parents and necking by the youngsters permitted in any seat in the house. Also free candy and popcorn to all!"

Reba and Bonnie Churchill
"Hollywood Earfuls," by Reba and Bonnie Churchill
Silver Screen, September, 1950

★　★　★

Ever since her puzzling break-up with Ronald Reagan, when Jane took a cruel emotional lacing and a great deal of second-guessing was printed as fact, only a few—a very few—have pierced the armor of her shyness. She steadfastly balks at talking about her home life, her children, her romances. Balks and explodes in four-letter vehemence.

Hollywood loves, of course, to type-cast everyone into a pattern: to squeeze you into The Mold. And when you refuse to be squeezed or molded, as Jane Wyman has refused, Hollywood screams in frustrated, childish anger.

Not long ago a gossip writer reported with some bewilderment that Jane Wyman had been seen in a skin-tight bathing suit tearing along Santa Monica beach with Clarke Hardwicke, her hair blowing about her face and she and Hardwicke laughing like "carefree kids." When the same reporter spotted Jane the following night at a preview, dressed in a severely tailored suit and squired by the non-social, serious-minded Lew Ayres, he was completely at sea. "This Wyman gal," he tsk-tsked, "won't fit into any pattern; she switches her personality with every man."

Foster James
"The Wyman Story," by Foster James
Motion Picture, November, 1950

★　★　★

I sincerely believe there's not a chance in the world of Jane Wyman and Ronald Reagan being married lovers again.

And, just as sincerely, I believe they will never be free of that perfect love they once shared.

I say, truthfully, that in my many years of reporting Hollywood love stories, I have never seen two people more deeply and excitingly in love than Jane and Ronnie back in those days when they first met.

I introduced them. You might say I practically threw them together when I invited them to come out with me on my first personal appearance tour twelve years ago. . .Ronnie, already a leading man at Warners, was my most "famous" name guest. Janie, still a stock player on the same lot, was making about $75 a week playing bits. Redheaded and ambitious Susan Hayward and Joy Hodges were also just starting.

Janie was openly and enthusiastically pleased at being invited along, and even before we opened our act in San Francisco it was obvious that she was especially pleased at being in such proximity to Ronnie, whom she considered a "famous star."

The January, 1943, cover of *Modern Screen*: Jane Wyman and Lieut. Ronald Reagan.

★ ★ ★

. . .Not long ago, I went to a dinner party at their home, and Maureen came in to cut her birthday cake. Her mother and father stood by her side, polite to each other and respectful—so different from those gay kids who went barnstorming with me. I turned away so they couldn't see the tears in my eyes.

Since then, when I see Janie, she seems self-sufficient, independent and oh, so gay. But I know that not long ago she said to someone, "What's the matter with me? I can't seem to pick up the pieces of my life again. Will I ever find happiness ahead?"

And, one of the lovely girls Ronnie seemed interested in for a while told me he recently said to her, "Sure, I like you. I like you fine. But I think I've forgotten how to fall in love."

Louella Parsons
"Are They Haunted by Their Perfect Love?"
by Louella Parsons
Modern Screen, February, 1951

★ ★ ★

Ronald Reagan and Nancy Davis at Ciro's. Their romance is a big thing.

Silver Screen
April, 1951

★ ★ ★

Ronnie Reagan, who has been dating Nancy Davis, told visitors to the set (of *Bedtime for Bonzo*) that he was quite resigned to the fact that the audience wouldn't even know he was in the picture. "When I went to the rushes all I looked at was Bonzo in spite of myself!"

Photoplay
April, 1951

★ ★ ★

No matter how you look at it, Ronald Reagan, the shy, quiet, executive-type actor, just *has* to be in love with Nancy Davis. Five will get you 10 anywhere in Hollywood that wedding bells will ring for them before many months have passed.

Nobody—especially Ronald Reagan—will forget the two-year parade of newspaper and magazine stories that had him eating his heart out for Jane Wyman; or the bulldog tenacity with which certain reporters stuck to that line long after Ronnie had passed the crisis and was having himself a time as a reconverted bachelor.

. . .They met in a rather official, although informal, manner. There was a vacancy on the board of directors of the Screen Actors Guild and, according to its policy of trying to get prominent players in office, it was decided to ask Nancy to accept the post.

Reagan, as president, was to make the formal call to Nancy. So he called and suggested that, since they didn't know each other, they meet across a plate of spaghetti or something. They've been looking at one another across something on a plate almost every night since.

It would be hard to find a girl more suited to Ronnie Reagan's somewhat split nature than Nancy Davis. She, too, has been tagged the serious type—mainly because of the roles she has so ably played in her MGM pictures. She comes from one of Chicago's first families. Her father is one of the world's most noted brain surgeons, and her mother is a

This is the Army (Warners, 1943), from Irving Berlin's all-soldier stage revue, provided Reagan (center) with one of his biggest screen successes. Sharing the scene above with him are George Murphy (also to be heard from politically), Joan Leslie and Charles Butterworth.

society leader. She has been educated in the finest schools and, actually, is not entirely in her element in the theatrical profession.

. . .In a wonderfully ordinary way, Nancy Davis has a great gift for home-making, a real attribute as far as a man of Reagan's tastes is concerned. Some time after she got her contract at MGM, she moved to an apartment in Westwood. That community has a group of sales developers which visits newcomers to the city and presents gifts from the local merchants, along with an invitation that the new resident drop in and say hello. It is purely a commercial proposition designed to build good will and attract new customers.

But Nancy Davis was so touched by the gesture that she was almost overcome with appreciation. She took the list of about 20 or 30 merchants, drove around to each one, thanked him for the gift and swore undying fidelity to his enterprise. She doesn't take even the simplest gesture of friendship lightly.

Jim Burton
"It Comes Up Love," by Jim Burton
Modern Screen, May, 1951

★ ★ ★

Ronald Reagan is just about the most romantic president the Screen Actors Guild ever elected to office.

Sidney Skolsky
"That's Hollywood for You," by Sidney Skolsky
Photoplay, May, 1951

★ ★ ★

Ronald Reagan and Nancy Davis (romantic twosome) exploring one of those "model homes"—for friends who are coming out from the East to settle here.

Cal York
"Inside Stuff," by Cal York
Photoplay, May, 1951

★ ★ ★

That Certain Party. All was Gold Medal and all glittered at *Photoplay's* annual Award Ceremony. This oldest award in the film industry which started way back in 1919 this year went to Betty Hutton and John Wayne for giving the most popular performances in 1950, and to *Battleground* as the most popular picture. Crystal Room impressions: Jane Wyman (with Greg Bautzer) being introduced by her good friend and ex-husband Ronald Reagan, who brilliantly emceed the brilliant affair. Janie, last year's winner, presented Betty Hutton's award to Paramount Vice President Y. Frank Freeman. Betty was in Florida.

Cal York
"Inside Stuff," by Cal York
Photoplay, May, 1951

★ ★ ★

The proceeds from Warners' *This is the Army* (1943), with Ronald Reagan and Joan Leslie,
went to Army Relief. Michael Curtiz, fresh from the Academy Award-winning *Casablanca*,
directed.

Dear Ronald Reagan:

According to newspaper reports, the Screen Actors Guild, of which you are president, plans this summer to launch a campaign to prevent fan magazines from running any stories about the private lives of established film stars. You implied that such stories might be all right for young actors on their way up, but that, once a person becomes a star, the only news that should be published about him ought to be stories which the star himself considers acceptable.

We think you should know that, regardless of what rules your organization sets up concerning what is and is not legitimate news for movie fans, every reporter and editor worth his salt is going to remember that his first responsibility is to his readers, and, in the good old American tradition, he is going to continue to print the legitimate news he thinks those readers want him to print.

What's legitimate news about a movie star?

The answer is virtually everything a star does or says. You are paid a large salary because you are a public figure. If you were an unknown, you could be just as handsome as you are now, just as good a performer and just as hard a worker. But your salary probably would be no bigger than that of a competent engineer, taxi-cab driver, machinist or manicurist, all of whom are just as accomplished in their professions as you are in yours. But their jobs don't depend on the size of their public.

Your made a personal appearance in Miami last winter to promote the box-office sale of your latest movie, *Storm Warning*. During that visit in Miami, everything you did was news—or it is assumed you wanted it to be so. Whether you made a visit to a veterans' hospital, addressed a luncheon or—should it have happened—engaged in a brawl in a night club, you must have expected to find something about in the papers next day, because that's why you were in Miami in the first place. But you should remember that you were news because publicity *made* you news.

You cited fan magazine stories about your divorce from Jane Wyman as "false and irresponsible invasions" of your privacy. We disagree. We disagree because you apparently didn't feel the marriage itself was a private affair (in 1943 our photographers were permitted to take all the pictures they wanted of your home, your wife and your family, and in 1941 you talked freely to our reporter concerning your expected baby, and posed buying toys, baby powder and bassinets). But, if the happy marriage was news, then it seems to follow that the *break-up* of that marriage also was news.

As for your reported feeling that publicity is all right for young actors, are we to assume you mean your fans are important to you only when you need them and that what you do once you gain stardom is none of their business?

Yours is a business, Mr. Reagan, which is built on publicity. In this sense, actors are like politicians; and, while Harry Truman could have written all the letters to music critics he wanted when he was a haberdasher in Missouri, once he became president such letters become news in every paper in the country. Although, since Mr. Truman's letter concerned his daughter, I imagine you felt his privacy had been invaded.

We suggest you take another look at your bank account, Mr. Reagan. And look around at your home, your present way of life, your success. If you decide they aren't worth the price you have to pay for them, then we think you've got a point. But, regardless of your

One from "The Gipper": Guest Ronald Reagan kisses the bride, Universal Pictures' exotic star Maria Montez, at her July, 1943, wedding to actor Jean-Pierre Aumont.

★ ★ ★

conclusions, as long as our readers are interested in Ronald Reagan, or any other important movie star, we're going to give them stories that satisfy that interest.

The Editors
Motion Picture, June, 1951

★　★　★

The only premiere I can think of this month was Universal–International's *Bedtime for Bonzo* at the Carthay Circle, which was somewhat marred by the accidental death of its chimpanzee star just the day before. For two hours before the screening, over fifty top animal actors were stalled in a midway erected outside the theater, where the public could see them for free. Later, several were brought on stage and awarded the Patsy (for best animal stars), which was accepted by their owner or trainer. Ronald Reagan presided and presentations were made by Jimmy Stewart, Diana Lynn, Rex Allen and other stars. Top honors went to Francis, the mule, star of the picture of the same name.

Grace Fischler
"Special Delivery from Hollywood," by Grace Fischler
Motion Picture, June, 1951

★　★　★

They spoke to each other over the phone, on a matter of business—Screen Actors Guild business—and Ronnie liked her voice. As for Nancy, she admired his "earnest manner," and thus began the romance of a couple who have no vices. Not for them the hot-house atmosphere of nightclubs, the smoky little rooms and the smell of Scotch. They eat at Dave Chasen's, they spend their evenings in the homes of friends, they drive along the Coast and look at the sea, they talk a lot and a lot of the time they're quiet. They go as "steady", according to one reporter, as any couple in Hollywood, and Nancy knits Reagan argyle socks, though she doesn't cook for him. (Her talent in the kitchen doesn't equal her talent before the cameras, concerning which her boss, Dore Schary, says, "She's a fine actress.") For Ronnie, whose last wife was bored by his serious attention to union matters, etc., Nancy's a good listener. For Nancy, Ronnie's the man she's been waiting for. Ask her if they'll marry, and she shakes her head no, but what, says everybody, is that lovely gleam in her eye all about?

Hollywood Yearbook
"Nancy and Ronnie: A Fine Romance—But Is It Love?"
1952

★　★　★

Actor Ronald Reagan and actress Nancy Davis were married yesterday in the Little Brown Church in the Valley by the Rev. John H. Wells, pastor of the San Fernando Valley church. The couple left by automobile for an undisclosed destination, but said that in a week they will go to Phoenix to join Mrs. Reagan's parents, Dr. and Mrs. Loyal Davis of

The October, 1944, cover of *Modern Screen*: Capt. Ronald Reagan.

★ ★ ★

Chicago. Reagan previously was married to Jane Wyman. The marriage was Miss Davis'
first.

The Los Angeles Times
March 5, 1952

★ ★ ★

I have never objected to talking to the press about my personal feelings for anyone. But I
have objected when a columnist or a writer puts words in my mouth or emotions in my
heart. At the time of my divorce I used to read the trash written about how I felt or Ronnie
felt and I just couldn't believe it. We were grown-up people with a serious problem and
we were painted as a couple of moony adolescents with absolutely no sense of responsibility.

   And during all that time nobody ever called me up and asked me for the facts. They just
came to conclusions and printed them.

Jane Wyman
"Lady Be Good," by Steve Cronin
Modern Screen, April, 1952

★ ★ ★

Recently, Jane had dinner with Ronald Reagan (her ex-husband) and his bride, Nancy.
Because of their children, Jane and Ronnie will always be friends.

Louella O. Parsons
"Louella O. Parsons' Good News"
Modern Screen, June, 1952

★ ★ ★

What happened to their love (Wyman's and Reagan's)? Both tried very hard to make the
marriage last, but I think it was simply that in maturing they grew apart in interests instead of closer. Finally the two children were their only tie.

   Happily they have maintained that mutual love for Maureen and Mike, and still confer
frequently about their welfare. Before Ronnie married Nancy Davis this year, he and
Janie had an occasional friendly date, which gave rise to those false rumors about reconciliation.

   Being a generous girl by nature, Jane naturally is glad that Ronnie has found happiness
again in a second marriage. For herself, however, she has no marriage plans right now.

Louella O. Parsons
"Hollywood's Ten Most Exciting Women"
by Louella O. Parsons
International News Service Story
October 24, 1952

★ ★ ★

During World War II (and despite its interruption of their lives), the Reagans rarely seemed
to stay home. Cameras caught them everywhere. Here they attend the California State
Military Guard Ball at the Hollywood Palladium. Mrs. Jack Benny is at far right.

Hollywood newlyweds Ronald Reagan and his lovely bride, Nancy Davis, had eyes only for each other as they enjoyed a honeymoon dinner at the Stork Club during New York visit.

Movie Time
"News and Notes"
October, 1952

★ ★ ★

Ronald's a rapid-fire talker, a habit acquired back when he was a sportscaster. . .Host of CBS-TV's *General Electric Theater*, he also is so busy in dozens of civic doings that he's on the phone for hours each day. . .Breeds horses on his 350-acre ranch. . .Big passion: politics. . .

TV Star Annual
1955

★ ★ ★

Reagan left home — briefly — this last year, to hop out to Las Vegas and get in on some of the gravy all the other Hollywood folks seemed to be pouring over themselves and finding a most warm, comforting bath. Ronnie had MC'd for nothing — free of charge, we mean — for so many years that it took him a while to realize he was grinning away a fortune. His act — a series of skits through which Ronnie was MC and fall guy, and personally stole the show with a "Beer Garden" number done with pantomime and a heavy accent — was a hit at The Last Frontier in Las Vegas, and London's Palladium contacted him about performing the same sort of chore across the sea, but he still hasn't made up his mind. . .Anyhow, he's busy with a television show now — *The G.E. Theater* — and he's been dutifully going around to all the plants of his sponsor, and talking to his fellow employees, which, according to columnist Sheilah Graham, "should boost his audience by a million or so."

Screen Album
May–July, 1955

★ ★ ★

Ronald and Nancy Reagan agree with people who marvel at their way of life — if turning your back on night clubs to sit home and play a quiet game of Scrabble is peculiar, then they're just about the oddest twosome in town! Not everybody thinks they have strange tastes. Many recognize the straightforward wisdom of the Reagan design for living.

Hollywood can be a terrifying trap for happy marriages; a trap baited with good times, gay nights and bleary mornings. Ask Ronnie — he's been caught in it once and doesn't intend to have it happen to him again. There's something about too many parties, too much rushing from entertainment to entertainment that undermines a good marriage, saps the very strength out of it. Nancy and Ronnie don't intend to have that happen to their precious marriage. That's why they have deliberately set up this off-beat, almost austere way of life. They dress simply, live in a house furnished comfortably but not elegantly.

Their happiest days are spent on their ranch, where Hollywood seems like the other side of the world. As soon as their daughter was born, they made a pact with each other to

Storm clouds had begun to gather for Mr. and Mrs. Ronald Reagan when this happy 1946 group picture was taken. Reagan, son Michael, Wyman and daughter Maureen in one of the recently adopted Michael's first family portraits.

★ ★ ★

keep her out of the spotlight, to keep her life sane and normal. That's why you've never seen pictures of adorable Patricia Ann. Has building this wall of simple living—unbelievably hard to do for Hollywood stars—paid off? Ronnie and Nancy know it has. They know their lives have a peacefulness, a serenity that few movie people can achieve. They are convinced this sense of normalcy adds new dimensions to their love. Most important to them, they see how Patty is developing—fairly blooming—in a home devoted to loving, family living. They look at Patty, look at each other, sigh happily and know that this Reagan way of life is the only one for them.

TV World
"Those Peculiar Reagans"
February, 1956

★ ★ ★

In June (1947) Ronnie got the flu and was in the hospital. Every day Janie came in to see him. "Honey," he protested, "do you think you should come here? After all, you're not the strongest."

"Of course I'm the strongest," Jane assured him. "The baby isn't due for three months. Stop worrying. I wouldn't miss a day with you for anything."

One day Jane missed a visit, and Ron knew something had gone wrong. That evening a friend came to see him.

"Something happened to Janie—what is it?" Ronnie asked.

The friend spoke softly. "Janie's all right. She'll be fine. But the baby, it came last night. A mite of a girl, just a pound and a half. The doctors did all they could. . ."

The loss of the baby was a shock Janie couldn't seem to cope with. She wanted to run away from all reminders—even Ronnie.

Nell Blythe
"Jane Wyman's Gamble with Happiness"
by Nell Blythe
TV Star Parade, May, 1957

★ ★ ★

Reagan, Irish-tempered and a devout believer in the rights of a husband, insisted that the marriage run his way, the story goes. Jane, at this point—according to insiders—unfortunately acted on the poor advice of industry friends and told Ronnie their marriage would have to give a little to her career. Ronald fought this as long as he could. Then he gave up.

So in 1948 they were divorced.

Modern Screen
September, 1957

★ ★ ★

Reagan, visiting Warners' commissary from the set of *Stallion Road* (1947), poses with starlet Martha Vickers (a future Mrs. Mickey Rooney), but—since he is still "happily married" to Jane Wyman and the darling of the fan magazines—he is careful not to be photographed sitting down with her.

Post-Production

A politician is one who talks himself red,
white and blue in the face.

CLARE BOOTHE LUCE

The 1960S

Ann Sheridan's films: "Torrid Zone," "They Drive By Night," "The Man Who Came to Dinner," "Nora Prentiss," "Good Sam," "I Was a Male War Bride" and four with Ronald Reagan: 1939's "Naughty But Nice" and "Angels Wash Their Faces," 1942's "Kings Row" and "Juke Girl."

That really surprised me (Ronald Reagan running for Governor of California).

I remember Ronnie telling all of us not to join TV because it was the enemy of the movies. Next thing, he was on *G.E. Theater* with his contact lenses reading the commercials.

Ann Sheridan
The Los Angeles Mirror, July 25, 1966

★ ★ ★

Nunnally Johnson wrote the screenplays for "Jesse James," "The Grapes of Wrath," "Tobacco Road," "Roxie Hart," "Woman in the Window," "Three Came Home," "How to Marry a Millionaire," "The World of Henry Orient" and "The Three Faces of Eve."

My defense of Ronnie Reagan (if I made one) was less out of an affection for actors than a sense of fair play. I resent a prejudice against minorities. It's all very well for you to dismiss actors as second-class citizens but the day may come when the streets will be red with blood as they rise up and demand ACTOR POWER! You can suppress a section of society only for so long. After all, they're paying taxes, some of them have developed qualities comparable even to those of writers, and it is only a question of time before the Screen Actors Guild springs to arms and will seize by force what they feel they are entitled to. This in fact may be the only hope of stopping Ronnie, for there are those who claim he is not really an actor but only passing. That's the worst sort, you know.

Nunnally Johnson
From letter to Shana Alexander in
The Letters of Nunnally Johnson
Alfred A. Knopf Publishers, 1981

★ ★ ★

Barbara Stanwyck co-starred with Ronald Reagan in the 1954 film "Cattle Queen of Montana." Her well-remembered films include: "Stella Dallas," "Remember the Night," "The Lady Eve," "Meet John Doe," "Ball of Fire," "Double Indemnity," "The Strange Love of Martha Ivers," "Sorry, Wrong Number" and "Titanic."

Ronald Reagan gives Jane Wyman fast xylophone lesson minutes before the August, 1946, broadcast of *Christmas in Connecticut* on the *Screen Guild* radio program.

★ ★ ★

This is the first time I've been kissed by a governor!

Barbara Stanwyck
Upon being presented the Screen Actors
Guild Achievement award by Governor-
elect Ronald Reagan at the Hollywood
Palladium in November, 1966

★ ★ ★

When Ronnie Reagan was actively pursuing his career as an actor, he was cast as a football hero, prisoner of war, football hero, alcoholic, football hero, horseman, etc., etc. But he was never cast as a governor, mayor, congressman or local dog-catcher. Obviously, the powers in charge didn't think he was "the type."

Hollywood Yearbook
"Now It's Reagan for President in 1968 (!!?!??!)"
1967

★ ★ ★

Foremost among Patricia Neal's films are "The Fountainhead," "Three Secrets," "The Day the Earth Stood Still," "A Face in the Crowd," "Hud," "The Subject Was Roses" and three with Ronald Reagan: 1949's "John Loves Mary" and "It's a Great Feeling" and 1950's "The Hasty Heart."

I don't like Ronald Reagan. If he runs for President or Vice President, I will give up my American citizenship, I really will.

Patricia Neal
United Press International Story
February 24, 1968

★ ★ ★

Jane Wyman's best starring films: "The Lost Weekend," "The Yearling," "Johnny Belinda," "The Glass Menagerie," "The Blue Veil," "So Big" and "Magnificent Obsession." Her films with Ronald Reagan: "Brother Rat" (1938), "Brother Rat and a Baby" (1940), "An Angel from Texas" (1940), "Tugboat Annie Sails Again" (1940), "It's a Great Feeling" (1949).

It's not because I'm bitter or because I disagree with him (Reagan) politically. I've always been a registered Republican. But it's bad taste to talk about ex-husbands and ex-wives, that's all. Also, I don't know a damn thing about politics. I don't care who does what to who and anyhow, now that I've moved into a new apartment, I live in a different district and I forgot to register, so I can't vote anyway.

Jane Wyman
"OK, So It's Not 'Johnny Belinda,' But. . ."
by Rex Reed
The New York Times, October 6, 1968

Reagan's first film released after his discharge from the service was *Stallion Road* (Warners, 1947), with Alexis Smith as love interest. He played a veterinarian.

*Curtis Bernhardt directed two films with Ronald Reagan: 1941's "Million Dollar Baby"
and 1942's "Juke Girl," as well as "My Reputation," "Devotion," "A Stolen Life," "Possessed," "The Blue Veil," Lana Turner's "The Merry Widow" and "Interrupted Melody."*

Then came a few things with our present governor here, Mr. Reagan. He was sort of an
unimportant, pleasant, typical, healthy American boy. You couldn't go wrong with him
in that kind of part. I don't like these films, and not only because of Mr. Reagan. One was
called *Juke Girl*, a sort of semi-Western laid among fruit-pickers and incorporating orgies
of fights; I don't know why they gave it to me. Another was *Million Dollar Baby*, with
Priscilla Lane.

Curtis Bernhardt
The Celluloid Muse, by Charles Higham and Joel Greenberg
Angus and Robertson Publishers, 1969

★ ★ ★

The three stars of *Stallion Road* (Warners, 1947) convene for a publicity picture: Ronald Reagan, Alexis Smith and Zachary Scott. Bogart and Bacall were originally announced for the film.

The 1970S

George Murphy, who in 1964 became U.S. Senator from California, was prominent in such films as "Little Miss Broadway," "Broadway Melody of 1940," "Little Nellie Kelly," "Tom, Dick and Harry," "For Me and My Gal," "Bataan," "Cynthia," "Battleground," "Talk About a Stranger" and with Ronald Reagan, 1943's "This is the Army."

One of the members of the S.A.G. board in the late thirties was a young contract player from Warners named Ronald Reagan. I didn't know him too well at the time. But I did admire his work, particularly in *Knute Rockne*.

I envied Reagan that part, but I must admit he did a superb job, one that practically made him a star overnight. In 1940, Ronald married a talented actress, Jane Wyman, and Julie (my wife) and I used to see them at parties. In those days we went to parties for fun, not publicity. Sunday nights we would all go over to Ann Sothern's where we would sing, dance or just tell stories. I sometimes danced so much at these parties that I'd go home wringing wet. But 1 loved it.

George Murphy
Say. . .Didn't You Used to Be George Murphy?
by George Murphy with Victor Lasky
Bartholomew House Publishers, July, 1970

★　★　★

Sheilah Graham was a Hollywood columnist and author of several volumes about her relationship with F. Scott Fitzgerald.

The Garden of Allah, the oasis for the intellectuals of Hollywood. . .The majority of the writers were left wing, as were some of the actors such as John Garfield, Edward G. Robinson, Freddie March and Ronald Reagan. Before he married Nancy Davis of Chicago, Ronnie was a strong liberal. Then he bacame just as staunch a Republican. Previously Ronnie had lived at the Garden after his divorce from Jane Wyman, and he was often in the bar talking politics by the hour.

Sheilah Graham
The Garden of Allah, by Sheilah Graham
Crown Publishers, 1970

★　★　★

Director Allan Dwan's credits include "Robin Hood" (with Douglas Fairbanks), "Heidi" and "Rebecca of Sunnybrook Farm" (both with Shirley Temple), "Suez," "Trail of the

That Hagen Girl (Warners, 1947) teamed teen-ager Shirley Temple (center) with thirty-six-year-old Ronald Reagan in one of the latter's least favorite films. Pictured at left is Jean Porter.

Vigilantes," "Sands of Iwo Jima" and two with Ronald Reagan: "Cattle Queen of Montana" (1954) and "Tennessee's Partner" (1955).

We shot *Cattle Queen of Montana* up in the Glacier National Park area of Montana. . .In those days, Ronald Reagan wouldn't fly. Neither would John Alton (the cinematographer). So they came to location by train—took them three days. We flew up in a couple of hours.

Reagan was a nice man, but he's got a temper. He's a good rider, but one time we got him on an Indian horse that wasn't broken and knew nothing about pictures. He was supposed to ride down toward the camera and warn somebody—he came tearing along on his horse, and as he approached the camera he was supposed to pull up and veer off. Well, as he started to, the horse began to dance sideways and he wound up way over there. And all the time Reagan is hollering, "Whoa! Whoa! Whoa!" As he went by the camera, he yelled out to me, mad as hell, "I'm not one of those Hollywood riders who says he can ride and can't ride! This goddamn horse won't do what I tell him!" He's explaining himself to me as he flies by the camera. Of course, we're howling with laughter.

Allan Dwan
Allan Dwan: The Last Pioneer, by Peter Bogdanovich
Praeger Publishers, 1971

★ ★ ★

Jack L. Warner was the pioneer movie mogul who ran Warner Brothers Studios and was Ronald Reagan's employer for fifteen years.

When Jack L. Warner returned to Hollywood in the mid-1960s from a European trip, a friend informed him that former Warner contract actor Ronald Reagan had been nominated to run for Governor of California. Replied Warner:

No, *no. Jimmy Stewart* for governor—Reagan for his best friend.

Jack L. Warner
The Wit and Wisdom of Hollywood, by Max Wilk
Atheneum Publishers, 1971

★ ★ ★

George Eells has written books on Cole Porter, Hedda Hopper and Louella Parsons, Anita O'Day, Mae West.

By Hedda Hopper's standards, Ronald Reagan had been foolishly liberal in his youth, but when he finally saw the light, he joined her list of patriots. Prior to his election as Governor, Hedda wrote a piece praising him; but her death occurred before his victory, and the article was not published.

Observing Hedda's success in cultivating political power, Louella Parsons plunged in and performed as adeptly as usual in areas alien to entertainment. Gazing into her

Reagan shared scenes with newcomer Lois Maxwell in *That Hagen Girl* (Warners, 1947). Maxwell is better known, however, for her continuing role as Miss Moneypenny in the James Bond films.

★ ★ ★

clouded crystal ball, she assured her readers that Ronald Reagan harbored no political ambitions.

George Eells
Hedda and Louella, by George Eells
Putnam Publishers, 1972

★ ★ ★

Alexis Smith's better films: "Gentleman Jim," "The Adventures of Mark Twain," "Conflict," "Night and Day," "The Woman in White," "Any Number Can Play," "Here Comes the Groom," "The Young Philadelphians" and 1947's "Stallion Road," opposite Ronald Reagan.

In retrospect everything looks so funny now. I remember playing a scene with the Governor of California (in 1947's *Stallion Road*). It called for a scene where we get off a horse and kiss under a tree. I was lying down in the grass and Ronnie lay down beside me and the director immediately yelled to him to get up on one elbow. "You both can't be in a prone position at the same time," he said, so Ronnie had to play the whole love scene on one elbow. How times have changed.

Alexis Smith
"One Last Look at Where It All Began"
by Craig Zadan
After Dark, February, 1972

★ ★ ★

Among Ray Milland's more than one hundred films: "Beau Geste," "I Wanted Wings," "Reap the Wild Wind," "Lady in the Dark," "The Big Clock," "Ministry of Fear," "The Uninvited," "The Lost Weekend," "Kitty" and "Love Story."

I attended a meeting of the full membership of the Screen Actors Guild held in the Hollywood Legion Stadium, and up in the ring presiding over it was the best president the Guild ever had, Ronald Reagan, now Governor of California. He had a tough job directing the traffic that night, what with calls to the barricades by a lot of coffeehouse characters, wailing about the violence outside studio gates. Hell, the only violent activity *I* ever saw outside a studio gate was over at Republic one morning, when Vera Hruba Ralston lost her skate key.

Ray Milland
Wide-Eyed in Babylon, by Ray Milland
William Morrow Publishers, 1974

★ ★ ★

Doris Day's many films include "Romance on the High Seas," "Tea for Two," "Calamity Jane," "Love Me or Leave Me," "The Man Who Knew Too Much," "The Pajama Game," "Pillow Talk," "That Touch of Mink" and two co-starring Ronald Reagan: 1951's "Storm Warning" and 1952's "The Winning Team."

One of Reagan's best films was the romantic comedy *The Voice of the Turtle* (Warners, 1947), opposite Eleanor Parker. It was based on the long-running John van Druten Broadway success that co-starred Margaret Sullivan and Elliott Nugent.

★ ★ ★

The city pounds, even the boarding kennels, are like concentration camps. . .We need legislation. . .I called Ronald Reagan and, of course, they said it was impossible to speak to the governor and I said, "You tell him it's his co-star from *The Winning Team*. I was married to him when he was only Grover Cleveland Alexander the baseball player, and he'd better call me back if he knows what's good for him." Well, he was on the phone in four minutes flat. I said, "Ronnie, this is Doris, and we're in big trouble down here in L.A.", and he said, "It's a city problem." He hates Mayor Yorty, and all these politicians do is shift the blame. But the animals suffer. Animals don't vote.

Doris Day
People Are Crazy Here, by Rex Reed
Dell Publishers, 1975

★ ★ ★

Ronnie is really the only man I've ever known who loved dancing. There was a little place on La Cienega that had a small band and a small dance floor where he often took me. He danced well and he had a pleasant personality.

When he wasn't dancing, he was talking. It really wasn't conversation, it was rather talking at you, sort of long discourses on subjects that interested him. I remember telling him that he should be touring the country making speeches. He was very good at it. . .He had what I would call a political personality—engaging, strong and very voluble.

Doris Day
Doris Day: Her Own Story, by Doris Day and A. E. Hotchner
William Morrow Publishers, 1975

★ ★ ★

James Cagney's best remembered roles: "The Public Enemy," "Footlight Parade," "G-Men," "Angels with Dirty Faces," "The Roaring Twenties," "The Strawberry Blonde," "Yankee Doodle Dandy," "White Heat," "Love Me or Leave Me," "Man of a Thousand Faces."

I got involved in a liberal group, the name of which I have mercifully forgotten. It had a leftist slant, was very well organized and made a point of recruiting celebrities, among them Ronald Reagan and myself. When Ronnie and I saw in which direction the group was headed, we both resigned the same night. From that time forth neither of us has looked back.

James Cagney
Cagney by Cagney, by James Cagney
Doubleday Publishers, 1976

★ ★ ★

Frank Westmore is the youngest of six brothers whose make-up mastery made the name of Westmore synonymous with Hollywood's "golden age."

My brother (Hollywood make-up pioneer Perc Westmore) cut and re-shaped Reagan's heavy thatch of hair (parting it on the left side), and consoled him when all his scenes in

Reagan liked to dance—off screen as well as on. Here, he cuts a conservative rug with co-star Eleanor Parker in *The Voice of the Turtle* (Warners, 1947).

his second movie, *Submarine D-1*, were considered so bad they were cut. . .For *Kings Row*, Perc himself made up all the stars, but he categorically refused to apply any make-up at all to Ronald's visage. And he had a battle royal over it with director Sam Wood. Perc said, "*I* am directing the make-up on this picture, and for the Reagan character to be believable, he cannot go around looking like a department store dummy." Perc won. And Ronald Reagan never forgot that his make-up artist friend, by *not* making him up, helped him stand out in one of his few memorable performances.

Frank Westmore
The Westmores of Hollywood
by Frank Westmore and Muriel Davidson
J. B. Lippincott Publishers, 1976

★ ★ ★

He (Ronald Reagan) was a liberal Democrat then (the late 1940s–early 1950s). It was amazing to all us Hollywood folks when he switched. They got to him. . .He married into a Republican family. I'm still liberal.

Doris Day
The Newark *Star-Ledger*
January 7, 1976

★ ★ ★

Bette Davis' many screen successes include "Of Human Bondage," "Jezebel," "The Old Maid," "The Letter," "Now, Voyager," "The Corn is Green," "Old Acquaintance," "Mr. Skeffington," "All About Eve" and, with Ronald Reagan, 1939's "Dark Victory."

Ronald Reagan gave no hint when we performed together at Warners (that he would become an aspirant to high political office). He was a very nice, pleasant little guy.

Bette Davis
The Mike Douglas Show (TV)
March 19, 1976

★ ★ ★

John Wayne's legendary career was highlighted by "Stagecoach," "Reap the Wild Wind," "They Were Expendable," "Red River," "She Wore a Yellow Ribbon," "Sands of Iwo Jima," "The Quiet Man," "The High and the Mighty," "The Alamo" and "True Grit."

The (Gerald) Ford administration has been giving Ronnie the (Barry) Goldwater treatment for a long time. They've tried to make him sound like a war-monger on Panama. Well, I've known Ronnie since he was President of the Screen Actors Guild and when he ran for Governor of California. He is no war-monger, so I decided not to be quiet about this.

John Wayne
United Press International Story
July 27, 1976

★ ★ ★

Reagan and the theater's Patricia Neal, in her screen debut, took over for originals William Prince and Nina Foch in the film version of Norman Krasna's New York stage hit *John Loves Mary* (Warners, 1949).

Evelyn Keyes' films: "Here Comes Mr. Jordan," "A Thousand and One Nights," "Renegades," "The Jolson Story," "The Mating of Millie," "Enchantment," "Mrs. Mike," "The Prowler," "The Seven-Year Itch," others.

One Sunday Ronald Reagan and his wife, Jane Wyman, dropped by. . .Bloody Marys seemed to be in order. . .The four of us piled in a car and took off for the Mexican quarter. John Huston, my husband, and Jane were drinking beer, but Ronnie and I had had enough, if indeed he had much of anything at all.

Jane and John, giggling and clearly anything but sober, were told to get in the back seat. "Evelyn and I will sit up front," said the future Governor of California. "We'll be the policemen, and I'll drive."

A sober-minded, responsible citizen, even then. A nice Democrat, then. I wonder where he went wrong.

Evelyn Keyes
Scarlett O'Hara's Younger Sister, by Evelyn Keyes
Lyle Stuart Publishers, 1977

★ ★ ★

Irving Rapper directed such films as "One Foot in Heaven," "Now, Voyager," "The Adventures of Mark Twain," "Rhapsody in Blue," "The Corn is Green," "The Glass Menagerie," "Marjorie Morningstar" and, with Ronald Reagan in 1947, "The Voice of the Turtle."

I had to smile when people told me how much they enjoyed *The Voice of the Turtle*, a comedy. I once told Hal Wallis, Warner Brothers' executive producer, "My friends think I should do comedy."

"No," he replied. "You're great in drama." And that, with one or two exceptions, has been what I've directed.

John van Druten, who wrote the stage hit *Voice of the Turtle*, was to have made his debut directing the film version. But he despaired when he realized the studio preferred to cast its own actors under contract. He therefore quit and asked Warners to let me direct it. But I, too, had a dream cast: Olivia de Havilland and Dana Andrews, who were then most popular. (Who could possibly take the place of Margaret Sullavan, the theater's original star?)

So I reluctantly accepted Ronald Reagan, whom no one took too seriously, and the lovely Eleanor Parker. I always believed that Eleanor, who was still relatively new, would become a star, and she didn't disappoint me. She was thoroughly professional and a great trouper. Even then, Ronnie had his sights on some political throne. Even after I yelled "Action!", he was still discoursing on Washington. Eve Arden I accepted with great enthusiasm. She rehearsed her hilarious scenes with meticulousness. She was always so serious you might have thought she was rehearsing Ibsen.

There's no such thing as an "easy" movie, but I must say that *Turtle*, of all the films I've done, *was* the easiest.

Irving Rapper
March 2, 1978

★ ★ ★

Warner Brothers stalwarts Wayne Morris, Ronald Reagan and Jack Carson in a scene from the farcical *John Loves Mary* (Warners, 1949), which had Patricia Neal (not shown) as feminine lead.

James Stewart's films: "You Can't Take It with You," "Mr. Smith Goes to Washington," "The Philadelphia Story," "It's a Wonderful Life," "The Stratton Story," "Harvey," "The Glenn Miller Story," "Rear Window," "Vertigo," "Anatomy of a Murder," and many more.

I campaigned with Ronnie Reagan through seven states on his last election and helped Eisenhower and Nixon with their campaigns, but I've never wanted to run for office.

James Stewart
"Talking on the Turnpike with My Father's Favorite Star"
by Arthur Bell
The Village Voice, August 14, 1978

★ ★ ★

Among Raymond Massey's films: "The Prisoner of Zenda," "The Hurricane," "Abe Lincoln in Illinois," "Reap the Wild Wind," "Arsenic and Old Lace," "Mourning Becomes Electra," "Possessed," "East of Eden" and two with Ronald Reagan: 1940's "Santa Fe Trail" and 1942's "Desperate Journey."

In *Santa Fe Trail*, Ronnie showed signs of the energy and initiative which made him such a good governor. . .The action was simply that the three troops mount and move off at the trot. Ronnie was holding forth about the direction. "This is a scene of action. We're too apathetic. There should be a feeling of urgency. We wouldn't mount formally by the drill book. I'm going to vault into the saddle and make it look like we're in a hurry." The other officers, including Errol Flynn, mindful of the potential discomfort of jumping into a McClellan saddle, indicated that they would do it as rehearsed.

"ACTION!" Ronnie sprang forward with a prodigious leap which carried him with his sabre in its sling to an ignominious landing on his behind on the other side of his horse.

Director Mike Curtiz shouted, "Cut! Acrobat bum!"

Raymond Massey
A Hundred Different Lives, by Raymond Massey
Little, Brown Publishers, 1979

★ ★ ★

Swedish star Viveca Lindfors' first American film was *Night unto Night* (Warners, 1949), opposite Ronald Reagan. Its downbeat themes of epilepsy and hallucinations kept it on the shelf for two years.

The 1980S

Hal Wallis, under whose production aegis (1930-44) many of Warner Brothers' most acclaimed films were made, was in charge of Ronald Reagan's "Brother Rat," "Dark Victory," "Knute Rockne, All American," "Kings Row" and "This is the Army."

Censor Joe Breen raised endless petty objections (to the script of *Kings Row*). He said we could not have a scene in which Drake McHugh said to his friend Parris, "You have to bunk with me. I hope you don't mind the change." We protested that these two men and the actors who played them, Ronnie Reagan and Robert Cummings, were entirely masculine and the line contained no suggestion of homosexuality, but Breen was adamant. We had to change the line to, "You have to bunk with me. I hope you won't mind, Mr. Mitchell!"

Hal Wallis
Starmaker: The Autobiography of Hal Wallis
by Hal Wallis and Charles Higham
Macmillan Publishers, 1980

★ ★ ★

Eddie Bracken co-starred with Ronald Reagan in 1949's "The Girl from Jones Beach"; was also in "Caught in the Draft," "The Fleet's In," "Star Spangled Rhythm," "The Miracle of Morgan's Creek," "Hail the Conquering Hero," "Out of This World," "Summer Stock."

Reagan was a lonely guy because of his divorce, but a very level-headed guy. He was never for the sexpots. He was never a guy looking for the bed. He was a guy looking for companionship more than anything else. But I wouldn't say he was straitlaced.

Eddie Bracken
"Non-Political Science: When Ronnie Was Running as a Bachelor"
by Rogers Worthington
Chicago Tribune, September 11, 1980

★ ★ ★

Leo Guild was a Warner Brothers publicist who made a 1944 U.S. Savings Bond promotion tour with, among other stars, Ronald Reagan.

The strange *Night unto Night* (Warners, 1949) failed, despite the earnest efforts of Reagan, Broderick Crawford, Viveca Lindfors and Rosemary De Camp. Latter, while slightly younger than Reagan, had played his mother in *This is the Army* (Warners, 1943).

When (John) Garfield and I were out chasing women, Reagan was in the hotel room studying scripts. He was a very serious man.

Leo Guild
"Non-Political Science: When Ronnie Was Running as a Bachelor"
by Rogers Worthington
Chicago Tribune, September 11, 1980

★ ★ ★

Doris Lilly appeared in the film "The Story of Dr. Wassell" but achieved note as a columnist and author. She dated Ronald Reagan in 1949-50.

He never went to the big parties at Selznick's or Joan Fontaine's. He made no effort in the direction of the glamour group.

He didn't care about society. He liked to be alone with you, having dinner, walking around New York.

He was discontented with films then. He made one really good picture, *Kings Row*. He was wonderful in it, and nothing happened. He should have gone from there to serious, good parts. But he wasn't willing to play up to people for parts he couldn't get on his own merits. He was too decent to be a big star.

. . .It wasn't hot and heavy, day in and day out. Ronnie wasn't a come-on strong type of man. He was never frantic about anything. I don't think he went with anybody for very long.

He is truly the all-American boy, never a lothario. . .I think that Ronnie, somehow, had a vision that he was saving himself for the big one. I think his restraint was much deeper than he realized. He behaved himself beautifully. He is a man who really needed to be with one woman.

Doris Lilly
"Non-Political Science: When Ronnie Was Running as a Bachelor"
by Rogers Worthington
Chicago Tribune, September 11, 1980

★ ★ ★

One of the 1940s' busiest leading men, Dennis Morgan acted with the first Mrs. Ronald Reagan, Jane Wyman, more than any other actor, including Reagan. The Morgan–Wyman movies: "Flight Angels," "Bad Men of Missouri," "Hollywood Canteen," "One More Tomorrow," "Cheyenne," "The Lady Takes a Sailor" and 1949's "It's a Great Feeling," in which Reagan also appeared.

He dated her (Betty Underwood) quite a bit, as I recall.

Dennis Morgan
"Non-Political Science: When Ronnie Was Running as a Bachelor"
by Rogers Worthington
Chicago Tribune, September 11, 1980

★ ★ ★

Lauren Bacall went on suspension at Warners rather than play the title role in *The Girl from Jones Beach* (Warners, 1949), so Virginia Mayo got to appear opposite the future President of the United States in a money-making movie.

Betty Underwood was a New York–based Powers model who appeared with Ronald Reagan in "The Girl from Jones Beach" (1949) and dated him during that period.

I can only say the nicest things about Ronald. He was a lot of fun, had a wonderful repertoire of jokes and was very good company. He was always up, and never at a loss for words. He was a wonderful connoisseur of wine.

I didn't date him very long. I lived in New York, and I only saw him in New York, except when I taught him how to water ski in Boca Raton, Florida. He was down there doing some appearances.

He was charming and delightful and very romantic. I'm sorry I threw away all the letters. I still have a telegram. The telegram mentions a song that was popular then, a song we shared some moments with: "The Third Man Theme."

Betty Underwood
"Non-Political Science: When Ronnie Was Running as a Bachelor"
by Rogers Worthington
Chicago Tribune, September 11, 1980

★ ★ ★

Col. Barney Oldfield, USAF (ret.), was a post–World War II Warner Brothers press agent who worked with Ronald Reagan, Jane Wyman, Errol Flynn and Ann Sheridan, among other stars.

There was a lot of talk (at a recent Hollywood party) about the flack-popular star, always a good interview, always loved to talk politics, was always the player to whom visiting potentates were taken.

He could put them at ease, talk well on many subjects and was interested in the world beyond Hollywood and the fan magazines.

That was the kid from Illinois and Iowa, Ronald Reagan. He has a road show of some size, the campaign for the Presidency.

Barney Oldfield
Daily Variety, October 14, 1980

★ ★ ★

Lee Grant's films: "Detective Story," "Middle of the Night," "Valley of the Dolls," "In the Heat of the Night," "The Landlord," "Portnoy's Complaint," "Plaza Suite," "Shampoo," "The Swarm," etc.

I don't know Reagan. I don't want to. I just hope we can get through the next four years alive.

Lee Grant
"Bell Tells," by Arthur Bell
The Village Voice, November 12-18, 1980

★ ★ ★

Silent screen star Lois Wilson made a comeback in a supporting role in *The Girl from Jones Beach* (Warners, 1949). Shown between scenes: Wilson, Ronald Reagan, the film's star (left), and its director, Peter Godfrey.

★ ★ ★

Among Ann Miller's many musical films: "Reveille with Beverly," "Easter Parade," "On the Town," "Texas Carnival," "Two Tickets to Broadway," "Lovely to Look At," "Small Town Girl," "Kiss Me, Kate," "Hit the Deck."

I think Ronnie would be just great (as President of the United States). I've known him and Nancy for years. He'll be a good change. *Miss Piggy* would be a good change.

Ann Miller
"Bell Tells," by Arthur Bell
The Village Voice, November 12-18, 1980

★ ★ ★

Ruth Warrick, star of the television soap opera "All My Children," appeared in such films as "Citizen Kane," "The Corsican Brothers," "Forever and a Day," "The Iron Major," "Mr. Winkle Goes to War," "China Sky," "Song of the South," "Daisy Kenyon" and "Arch of Triumph."

I know why the polls were way off. Everyone was ashamed to admit they'd vote for Reagan, then went right ahead and did.

I knew Ronnie during my Hollywood days. He didn't talk: he pontificated, even then. He was a terrific salesman, and he believed the homilies he spouted.

Ruth Warrick
"Bell Tells," by Arthur Bell
The Village Voice, November 12-18, 1980

★ ★ ★

Philip Dunne's screenplays: "The Rains Came," "How Green Was My Valley," "The Late George Apley," "Forever Amber," "The Ghost and Mrs. Muir," "Pinky," "David and Bathsheba," "The Robe," "Ten North Frederick," many more.

In 1965, I went to Universal Studios to write and direct a serio-comic spy melodrama called *Blindfold*, starring Rock Hudson. The picture itself was unimportant, but it spawned a by-product which may have exerted an extraordinary influence on national affairs.

We were having trouble casting the "heavy," an unscrupulous spy master in the pay of an unspecified Communist government. Since it was a comedy, we didn't even give our villain a dignified comeuppance at the end: he was kicked into quicksand by an intelligent mule.

My old friend Bob Arthur, who sat on the political spectrum about as far to the right as I did to the left, was the executive producer. He was also a close friend of Ronald Reagan's. Arthur dropped in at my office one morning and said, "Phil, I had no right to do this without consulting you, but I showed the script to Ronnie last night and he's dying to play the part. He's tired of playing the hero's best friend and thinks he can make a new career for himself as a heavy."

I said, "Oh, come on, Bob. Ronnie's all wrong for the part. Audiences have typed him as a good guy—the all-American middle-aged Boy Scout. They'd never buy him as a heavy. He won't frighten anybody." We cast a different actor.

Reagan (in chair, right) made a guest appearance in the all-star *It's a Great Feeling* (Warners, 1949), as did Jane Wyman and daughter Maureen. Since he and Wyman were divorcing, they did not appear together on screen. Also here: Wendy Lee, Jack Carson, Cosmo Sardo, Ed Agresti and Howard Washington.

A few months later, we were off on location in a Florida cypress swamp and, at about the time our trained mule kicked this other actor into the quicksand, we heard on the radio that, back in California, Ronald Reagan had announced his candidacy for the governorship.

Philip Dunne
Take Two, by Philip Dunne
McGraw-Hill Publishers, 1980

★ ★ ★

Ila Rhodes worked with Ronald Reagan in the late-1930s films "Secret Service of the Air," "Dark Victory" and "Hell's Kitchen."

I was twenty-one, and he was around thirty, tall and cute. Ronnie was very attractive, and I didn't take any antidote to ward off this attraction. . .We made "B" films. . .The short time we filmed together led to lunch-break trysts and weekends out together, snatched from a hectic Hollywood schedule. . .I became engaged to him, with a ring on my finger. . .In all, the engagement lasted eight or nine months, when the studio decided romance between their stars was bad for boxoffice business.

Ila Rhodes
New York Post, December 18, 1980

★ ★ ★

Viveca Lindfors, who starred in "Anastasia" on Broadway, has appeared in such films as "Adventures of Don Juan," "No Sad Songs for Me," "Run for Cover," "I Accuse!", "Weddings and Babies," "King of Kings," "No Exit," "The Way We Were," "Creepshow" and, opposite Ronald Reagan, "Night unto Night" (1949).

Night unto Night was not the perfect set-up. The formula was to match a new foreign girl (me) with a big American star. Ronald Reagan was not that. . .I don't remember a single conversation with him of any substance. I do remember some chitchat about sex, which was up my alley. "It's best in the afternoon, after coming out of the shower," he said, and then he laughed the same, slightly embarrassed laugh that he did on TV the other day. Nancy was sitting listening to him during the speech. I kept thinking, "Does he still like it in the afternoon? Does she? I hope so!"

Viveca Lindfors
Viveka. . .Viveca, by Viveca Lindfors
Everest House Publishers, 1981

★ ★ ★

Among Piper Laurie's films: "The Prince Who Was a Thief," "Has Anybody Seen My Gal?", "No Room for the Groom," "Mississippi Gambler," "Until They Sail," "The Hustler," "Carrie" and, in 1950, "Louisa," starring Ronald Reagan.

Reagan and Patricia Neal arrive in the United States aboard the Queen Mary in 1949 after filming *The Hasty Heart* (Warners, 1950) in England. Neal's comments over the years indicate a pronounced love-hate relationship with Reagan.

My first move was *Louisa*. Ronald Reagan played my father. He also took me to my first premiere. I was so excited to be out with an older man that I forgot the name of the movie.

Piper Laurie
New York Post, January 27, 1981

★ ★ ★

William Holden's films: "Golden Boy," "Sunset Boulevard," "Stalag 17," "Sabrina," "The Country Girl," "Love is a Many-Splendored Thing," "Picnic," "The Bridge on the River Kwai," "Network," etc.

Reagan's a good friend, or was. Deep down, he's basically decent, but we don't necessarily agree on issues. Still, no reason to let that come between us. He used to be a lot of fun.

William Holden
The Merv Griffin Show (TV), 1981

★ ★ ★

He was a silly young kid. Everyone called him Little Ronnie Reagan.

Bette Davis
Good Morning America (TV)
May 14, 1981

★ ★ ★

I think he's (Reagan) doing a marvelous job. I really do. We're very good friends and I just adore him. Thank God he's alive. That was a very dramatic thing (Reagan's shooting by John Hinckley, Jr.).

Jane Wyman
"Liz Smith"
New York *Daily News*, June 9, 1981

★ ★ ★

Ronald Reagan was supposed to be running away from, or after, Virginia Mayo in *The Girl from Jones Beach* and I was in hot pursuit of Dona Drake. I came up with the idea for a comedy bit where we'd get confused and chase the wrong girl for a minute or two, then turn around and bump into each other. That's when Ronnie broke some of his vertebrae.

Just about the same time, Ronnie invited me out to a ranch and decided I should learn to ride. Well, I'm petrified of horses. He decided to show me how easy it was. Well, he fell off and broke some ribs.

And it doesn't end there. After the President was shot, I saw a picture of him on television getting off a plane from Camp David. The commentator mentioned that he seemed to be limping, but that it was "from an old injury." I began to wonder about the time I organized the Movie Star World Series. The idea was to have all the big Hollywood stars play in the baseball stadiums around the country to help raise money for the City of Hope.

Reagan and Patricia Neal teamed for the second time in the screen translation of Broadway's *The Hasty Heart* (Warners, 19 50), which on the stage had featured John Lund and Anne Burr in their roles. Co-star Richard Todd got the Academy Award nomination, but Reagan was praised.

Well, the day of the first game at the old Wrigley Field in L.A., my car stopped at a traffic light in Beverly Hills, and who rolled up beside me but Ronnie and Nancy. I had asked him to play in the opening game, forgetting he was still getting over his injury. I hollered out to him, "Hi, Ron. Are you on the way to the game?" He looked a little embarrassed and said, "Well, I can't."

I get to the ballpark, and who's waiting for me at the gate but Ronald Reagan. I told him, "Ronnie, I was only kidding when I zoomed away in the car. After all, I'm the guy who did it to you." He said he was glad to be there and we put him up to bat first, so that he could go home early. Bob Hope was pitching and Ward Bond was catching. I was in the infield.

Ronnie hit the ball and started running for first. He tripped and they had to carry him off the field. He had broken a leg. To this day, when I go up and say, "Hiya, Ronnie," his hand comes up defensively in front of him.

By the way, many of the big names cancelled out of the rest of the Movie Star Series because the studios were afraid of injuries after Ronnie broke his leg.

Eddie Bracken
"Bracken Recalls Run-in with Ronnie"
by William A. Raidy
The Newark *Sunday Star-Ledger*, June 28, 1981

★ ★ ★

Fred de Cordova, producer of TV's "The Tonight Show Starring Johnny Carson," has directed many films, including "Her Kind of Man," "Wallflower," "The Countess of Monte Cristo," "For the Love of Mary," "Here Come the Nelsons" and, most notably, 1951's "Bedtime for Bonzo," starring Ronald Reagan.

As you can imagine, I have been asked on many occasions to discuss *Bedtime for Bonzo* and Mr. Reagan's participation in it. It was a delightful experience, and he was, to say the least, an extremely dedicated and competent performer. He was a director's delight — always on time, always totally prepared and extremely cooperative. We have remained friends over the years. Both the President and Mrs. Reagan are charming and considerate. When my wife and I went to Washington for the inauguration, the Reagans — even in those hectic days — were as kind and considerate as they had been before the election.

Fred de Cordova
July 7, 1981

★ ★ ★

Stephen Longstreet wrote the screenplay for "Stallion Road" (1947), starring Ronald Reagan. He also wrote the book for the Broadway musical "High Button Shoes" and co-wrote the films "The Jolson Story" and "Silver River."

Ronald Reagan was and is a decent person — not an intellectual, though. In the seven years I was at Warner Brothers and knew him there, I found much to like in the man. He saw, and still sees, everything as very simple.

Going by his actions, he believes that the rich have the right life and the right ideas on

Ronald Reagan, circa 1950.

how to run the country. When I worked with him, it was clear he was a man escaping from the memories of boyhood poverty to run with the present palace guard.

Stephen Longstreet
July 10, 1981

★ ★ ★

Rosemary DeCamp is remembered for "Hold Back the Dawn," "Jungle Book," "Yankee Doodle Dandy," "Pride of the Marines," "Rhapsody in Blue," "Nora Prentiss," "Night into Morning," "On Moonlight Bay" and two films with Ronald Reagan: 1943's "This is the Army" and 1949's "Night unto Night."

With Ronald Reagan, it is now difficult to separate the man from his politics. I am very wary of Reagan reminiscences. I love his brother Neil, having worked for him on radio's *Dr. Christian* and, for two decades, *Death Valley Days*.

In the 1943 film *This is the Army* I played Ronnie's mother. (It is, by the way, a wonderful musical with great stars, music and pace.) He was handsome, laughing, loaded with charm—just as he is now. During *Night unto Night*, made during part of 1946 and 1947 (but not released until 1949!), and in which we again acted together, he worked eighteen to twenty hours a day: at night, trying to resolve an ugly industry strike as he was the President of the Screen Actors Guild; then all day on that baffling film about a man with epilepsy. But he remained cheerful and loquacious with three or four hours of sleep a night. This went on for months and may have been the cause of his divorce from Jane Wyman, who must have had a difficult and lonely time as Mike and Maureen were very young.

The twelve years I was on the SAG (Screen Actors Guild) Board when Reagan was its President gave us all a realization of what a firm, dogged negotiator he was. We won the principle of Payment for Re-use in TV. All of us who sat around that bargaining table, however, sacrificed careers at the major studios. Jack Warner, Spyros Skouras, Darryl Zanuck and Y. Frank Freeman had long memories.

My disillusionment with Reagan thinking occurred to the endless repetitions of his recorded voice in my doctor's waiting room. He told us Medicare would sweep this country into bankruptcy. . .by all means stop the King–Anderson Bill which would provide funds for the sick, the elderly and the disadvantaged.

This couldn't be the same man who had fought for the workers in our union! What had become of the compassion and understanding he had shown then?

Now as President of our country he is even more charming and likeable as a speaker. But when you analyze what he says. . .it is the voice of Business. . .Oil. . .Conglomerates. . .Munitions. . .and above all Money. . .Government is Business not People.

Rosemary DeCamp
July 14, 1981

★ ★ ★

Joy Hodges Schiess, as Joy Hodges, performed in such 1930s films as "Follow the Fleet," "Merry-Go-Round of 1938," "Service de Luxe," "They Asked for It," "Little Accident," "Laughing at Danger" and 1940's "Margie." She starred on Broadway in the 1970s revival of "No, No, Nanette."

A rare photo of Ronald Reagan wearing eyeglasses in public. In country costume for a 1950 "Whoop De Do" Hollywood benefit are actresses Jeanne Crain and Ann Blyth, actor Richard Long, Paul Brinkman, Crain's husband, and Reagan.

Some personal thoughts on my friend Ronald Reagan, our beautiful President. . .

I dislike appearing to take too much credit for the change which came about in Reagan's life, although *he* is certainly one never to forget a kindness.

Just *imagine* if I had kept the note he sent backstage when I was singing with the Jimmie Grier band asking me to come out at intermission time to say hello. That was at the Baltimore Bowl in Los Angeles. Years later he sent me a beautiful letter on the afternoon of his first vote as Governor of California. It reads in part: "Just think, tonight I will be sitting in the same room awaiting the results of the voting, the same room where you so graciously gave me that gentle push so many years ago."

The "gentle push" occurred during our conversation at a Biltmore table back in 1937. He said he would like to go through a studio the next day. (This was Friday night; he was leaving Monday night for Des Moines, Iowa, where I first met him—more on this later.) I said I thought it could be arranged, but then he said, "If you really want to know, I'd like to get a screen test."

Now comes the important part. I don't know whether I wanted him to think I had the pull to get him a screen test or what, but I said, "Stand up." (The show was going on and there was music blaring away.) When he stood, he was so tall and so good-looking, but with those awful horn-rimmed glasses on. I said, "Take off those glasses!", which he did, and I told him, "Don't ever put them on again." I don't think he ever has—publicly. Well, I asked him to call me at nine the next morning and told him I would call my agent very early, which I did.

George Ward, who worked for the Bill Meiklejohn Agency, was my agent. I gave George a big, fast sales pitch and he said to have Ronnie call him immediately. They met and went to the studio. George can tell you the rest. I understand "Dutch" (as Ronnie was called) really "snowed" Max Arnow, the casting director, with his fantastic gift of gab.

Ronnie and I rehearsed Sunday, Monday he made the test and Thursday he was back in California. I was beside myself with joy and sent a telegram to the Des Moines *Register* and *Tribune* telling them they had a big star in their midst. Somehow I knew that Des Moines and radio station WHO had seen the last of him as a sportscaster.

This is how we really met. . .

I had made a short film with Jimmie Grier and got a contract at RKO, although I made only about three pictures in six months. The first was another short in which I had one line—"Junior forgot to eat his spinach"—and walked in leading a horse. I was the maid. Well, when it played my home town, Des Moines, you can imagine—I was in the MOVIES, with headlines trumpeting that I was coming home for a personal appearance. When I arrived, WHO Radio called for an interview.

So, I was at the mike there and in walked this tall, handsome young man wearing a riding outfit, a huge smile and glasses. We were just going on the air, and he ad-libbed, "Well, Miss Hodges, how does it feel to be a movie star?" I was embarrassed but I flipped back, "Well, Mr. Reagan, you just may know some day." Now why in the world would I say that?! I honestly think there was some kind of intuitive message between us—the same kind of message that prompted me to say "Why not?" later when he mentioned the screen test, instead of "Are you kidding?"

He remembered me when he came to Los Angeles—and the rest is truly history.

About my attitude towards him. . .

We were never anything to each other but the very warmest of friends. I love him with all my heart because he is one of the most honest, compassionate, warmest, simplest of men. (Yes, "simplest," although you might not think so now considering the social group with which he has identified, but that is Nancy's wish and he adores her and happily has gone along with many of her ambitions for him. He wouldn't have made it without her, I am sure; she polished him and exposed him to the life which moulded him and readied

Louisa (Universal, 1950) was a light story of love among the elderly—no, not Ronald Reagan this time. His love interest was a still spry Ruth Hussey, but the focus was on the venerable players Charles Coburn, Edmund Gwenn and Spring Byington.

him for where he is now.) He never forgets. He has the capacity to stop and stand back and look at a situation — good or bad — as if he were not involved in it. He has only the ego required of him at the moment.

I used to think he was a real college boy when he would sit and sing college songs as we were riding in the bus when we went on a vaudeville tour with Louella Parsons in 1939; but it was all his way of pulling us out of the awful boredom. We were always together then, all of us, and sometimes tempers flared, but there was never a flare-up between "Dutch" and anybody. He was the happy catalyst, the only man in the Parsons troupe which also included his girlfriend, Jane Wyman. There was a stage manager, but the girls all went to "Dutch" with any problem. He and Jane were planning on getting married, but they were very discreet and he was as attentive to the rest of us as to her.

He knows he is not the most brilliant man alive; consequently, he surrounds himself with those he trusts. When a problem comes up, I know he prays, but he doesn't claim to be a born-again anything. He is quiet and rather shy about the most personal subjects in his life. I admire him. I don't agree with him on abortion — I believe in the right of women to choose. I think life begins when it appears and it is not murder to abort a fetus. Unlike him, I believe in gun control — registration of guns and the most severe sentence if anyone is murdered with a gun. But all in all, I know he is doing what his little angel on his shoulder is telling him to do.

I saw him a year ago March in Westchester, New York, at a Republican fund-raising dinner. He knew we would be there. He was at one end of the corridor and my husband and I at the other. When he saw me, he made a running advance from one end and I did likewise from the other, both with arms open. He flung me up and hugged me while the Secret Service men were urging him on. He said, "Just a minute. If it weren't for this lady I wouldn't be standing here." They couldn't have cared less. My darling husband Eugene walked up and said, "Hello, Governor. I'm the other half of this hysterical team." "Dutch" laughed and nearly hugged Gene.

As he sat at the table on the dais that night, several times he was alone as the local politicians were doing their thing. Gene leaned over and said to me, "Look at that. There sits the next President of the United States — alone!" We couldn't go up, but I had a letter from him later apologizing for not seeing us afterwards. Of course we had not expected that.

I have the greatest respect for him. I am so sad to have lost that personal touch. The letters now are from expert secretaries. Nancy didn't answer my letter to her when the President was shot, but she, as we all were, was devastated.

Joy Hodges Schiess
July 22, 1981

★ ★ ★

Lee Patrick's several dozen films include "City for Conquest," "The Maltese Falcon," "Now, Voyager," "Mrs. Parkington," "Mildred Pierce," "Mother Wore Tights," "The Snake Pit," "Caged," "Vertigo" and, with Ronald Reagan, 1941's "Million Dollar Baby."

Although I appeared in *Million Dollar Baby,* in which Ronald Reagan had one of the leads, I never met him. We had no scenes together.

This was not unusual, the way pictures were made in those days. I never met Jimmy Cagney and I was in *City for Conquest* with him. The same goes for Paul Henreid in *Now, Voyager.*

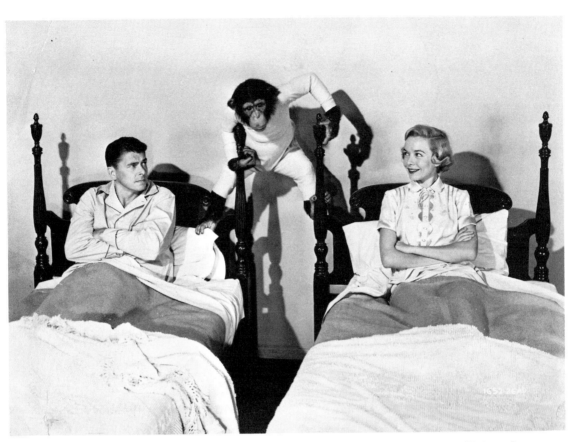

The film Ronald Reagan will never be allowed to live down: *Bedtime for Bonzo* (Universal, 1951). The future President of the United States played straight to a chimpanzee in a cast that also included Diana Lynn.

I must say, though, that I have great respect and admiration for our President, for when he was President of the Screen Actors Guild he pushed through the pension plan for actors. I am certainly enjoying mine.

Those who worked in scenes with Ronald Reagan used to say that he was like Clark Gable, a complete pro. I feel that is the finest compliment that can be paid any actor.

Lee Patrick
July 24, 1981

★ ★ ★

Theodore Bikel's films: "The African Queen," "The Divided Heart," "The Defiant Ones," "I Want to Live!", "My Fair Lady," "My Side of the Mountain." He was Mary Martin's leading man in "The Sound of Music" on Broadway.

Regarding President Reagan's proposed budget cuts to the arts: Every profession has its John Wilkes Booth. Reagan is ours.

Theodore Bikel
People, 1981

★ ★ ★

Vincent Sherman has directed "The Hard Way," "Old Acquaintance," "Mr. Skeffington," "Nora Prentiss," "Adventures of Don Juan," "Harriet Craig," "Goodbye My Fancy," "The Young Philadelphians" and in 1950, "The Hasty Heart," starring Ronald Reagan.

The Hasty Heart was one of my most enjoyable experiences as a director. Ronald Reagan, Richard Todd and Patricia Neal were the stars. Richard was nominated for an Academy Award; although he didn't win it, his performance was appreciated by many. Our President also did one of his best acting jobs.

As for my relationship with Ronald Reagan, it covered a long period. We both began at Warner Brothers in 1937, he as a young actor appearing mostly in "B" films and I starting as a writer on "B" films. Our paths crossed several times, once when I "picked up" (directed) a shot of him doing a radio broadcast for some film that I have forgotten, and once when I did some retakes for another director on *Juke Girl*, in which he starred. He was always pleasant to work with and highly professional.

Later, he graduated to roles in "A" films and I became a director. While we were never very close, I think we always had a mutual respect for each other. He was well informed about many subjects and it was a kind of joke around the lot that he could expound on almost anything, and frequently did. Some considered him a walking encyclopedia.

My first really intimate experience with Ronnie came during the making of *The Hasty Heart*. As I recall, he had really hoped to play the more dramatic part of the Scot, "Lachie," which Richard Todd played, but Jack Warner wanted him to play "Yank." He *did* have a long, tough struggle at Warners in his effort to get interesting and meaningful roles. I think this was because, when he started, he was considered simply a nice American young man who used to be a radio announcer. We were in London for almost six months making *Heart*, during one of the coldest and most bitter winters ever in England. (And our story was set in a hot Burmese jungle!) A chauffeur would pick him up at the Savoy Hotel, along with Patricia Neal, then pick up Todd and myself for an hour's journey to the

Ronald Reagan played the D.A., Ginger Rogers, a Ku Klux Klan victim in *Storm Warning* (Warners, 1951). The film's social overtones did not obscure its plot debt to the contemporary Broadway and film hits *A Streetcar Named Desire*.

studio at Elstree. Some mornings the fog was so heavy it would take us two or three hours to get there.

Beyond the time we spent at the studio shooting, which was almost every day except Saturday and Sunday, I didn't see too much of him but I think he used to attend the soccer matches and visit various points of interest. When we first arrived in London we spent an evening or two together and he told me about his recent divorce from Jane Wyman, and from what I could gather, it hurt him considerably. We also had some lively political discussions. He had at one time been a liberal Democrat, then after the war his politics began to move toward the right. I was, I suppose, a liberal, left-wing Democrat. I'm sorry to say that on some issues, especially regarding the Soviet Union, he was more correct than I was.

My experience in directing him was most pleasant. He was easy to work with, always knew his lines, was conscientious and took direction. Because of his American boyish good looks he was probably deprived of playing some of the more colorful roles which came up, but this same quality is what also helped to get him elected President.

I haven't seen or spoken to him in years, but I've watched his progress and he has become a skillful and appealing politician. He is, I think, basically honest, and I think he believes what he says, although I don't agree with many of his statements.

I wish I could give a more colorful account, but Ronnie was a well-behaved, easygoing, professional actor who was never involved in any serious scandal or Hollywood pecadillo. This does not make for an exciting personality, but if he does a good job as President who cares whether he is exciting.

Vincent Sherman
July 25, 1981

★ ★ ★

Tex Swan, a bit player and extra in many Hollywood films, supported Ronald Reagan in 1940's "Knute Rockne, All American."

I did seven movies with Jane Wyman, including *Johnny Belinda* and *Magnificent Obsession*, and I worked with Ronald Reagan, too. I had a minor role in *Knute Rockne, All American*. Reagan was the most appreciative guy in the world. He was so glad to be there instead of some little radio station in Nebraska.

Tex Swan
Asbury Park Press
July 26, 1981

★ ★ ★

Dorothy Tree was featured in "Confessions of a Nazi Spy," "Charlie Chan in The City of Darkness," "Abe Lincoln in Illinois," "Edge of Darkness," "No Sad Songs for Me," "The Asphalt Jungle," "The Men" and with Ronald Reagan, 1940's "Knute Rockne, All American."

I've long since forgotten a good deal of my Hollywood past. Today I write and teach. I cannot recall accurately a film like *Knute Rockne, All American*, made forty years ago, and would need to see it again. I only recall that I played the mother of Knute Rockne who was played by Pat O'Brien. Ronald Reagan and his role in it remain nebulous to me.

Ronald Reagan attended the after-Oscar party at the Beverly Hills Hotel following the 1951 Academy Awards with date Nancy Davis, but is shown above chatting with Ava Gardner, who was escorted by hairdresser Sidney Guilaroff.

As for the astonishing rise of Ronald Reagan, politician. . .I served on the board of the Screen Actors Guild from 1937 to 1946, and Mr. Reagan was, of course, quite active in it. He was beginning his political climb then. Trade unionism was the impetus. His politics were liberal then. He was to the left of Robert Montgomery, who preceded him as President of the Guild, and an agreeable guy, given to anecdotes. He showed little of the future man. Years later, he switched to the corporations and stumped the territory for General Electric. The rest you know.

Dorothy Uris (Dorothy Tree)
July 29, 1981

★ ★ ★

Actress Dorothy Adams, widow of the veteran character actor Byron Foulger, brightened dozens of films, including "Ninotchka," "So Proudly We Hail," "Laura," "The Best Years of Our Lives," "Sentimental Journey," "Carrie," "The Big Country." She portrayed Ronald Reagan's mother in 1952's "The Winning Team."

I remember Ronald Reagan as being gregarious, very friendly and outgoing. He enjoyed his work, whatever he had to do. If anything went wrong, such as flubbing a line, etc., he laughed about it and it was simply done again. He loved jokes—both hearing them and telling them. He always seemed to have a good time on the set. Certainly he was *not* one of those serious young actors who kept himself aloof. He was enthusiastic and, I would say, eager to be successful. I think he enjoyed the teamwork involved in filmmaking.

I wish you success with your research on Ronald Reagan's film career. He is certainly making great headway in his Presidential one.

Dorothy A. Foulger (Dorothy Adams)
August 8, 1981

★ ★ ★

Laraine Day was heroine in seven Dr. Kildare features, plus "My Son, My Son," "Journey for Margaret," "Mr. Lucky," "The Story of Dr. Wassell," "The Locket," "Tycoon" and 1941's "The Bad Man," opposite Ronald Reagan.

Reagan once told me some advice Bill Holden gave him that he said changed his life: "Don't be jealous of other people, don't resent other people getting good parts.". . .I think Ronnie wanted to be President many years ago. . .When he made it, I sent a congratulatory telegram. Two days later the phone rang and it was the President-elect. The first thing he said to me was a line from the opening of our scene in *The Bad Man*—"I have a little going-away present for you." I couldn't believe he remembered it. . .He was always more interested in politics than acting. He was so involved, so dedicated, there was no other place for him to go.

Laraine Day
People, August 10, 1981

★ ★ ★

Bedtime for Bonzo (Universal, 1951) was directed by Fred de Cordova, who went on to be producer of *The Tonight Show Starring Johnny Carson* on television. Reagan and Diana Lynn starred, but Bonzo the chimp stole the show.

★ ★ ★

H. Bruce Humberstone directed "Sun Valley Serenade," "I Wake Up Screaming," "Hello, Frisco, Hello," "Pin-Up Girl," "Wonder Man," "Three Little Girls in Blue," "The Desert Song," and 1952's "She's Working Her Way Through College," starring Ronald Reagan.

When Reagan re-wrote his big speech in *She's Working Her Way Through College*, Jack Warner came storming onto the set and said to me, "What's this I hear about you letting a damned actor write his own speeches?" But then he listened to Ronnie's version and said, "You win."

H. Bruce Humberstone
People, August 10, 1981

★ ★ ★

Dorothy Malone's films: "The Big Sleep," "One Sunday Afternoon," "Battle Cry," "Written on the Wind," "Man of a Thousand Faces," "The Tarnished Angels," "Too Much Too Soon" and, opposite Ronald Reagan, 1953's "Law and Order."

I liked the Ronald Reagan I acted with a lot better than the one who is now in the White House. . .I'm not in any tax bracket that any tax cut would help. He has let the gasoline prices go up so that I can hardly afford to drive. My parents are in a nursing home, and we cannot afford one little dollar cut in Medicare.

Dorothy Malone
People, August 10, 1981

★ ★ ★

Virginia Mayo, who co-starred with Ronald Reagan in 1949's "The Girl from Jones Beach" and 1952's "She's Working Her Way Through College," also did "The Princess and the Pirate," "The Best Years of Our Lives," "The Secret Life of Walter Mitty," "White Heat," "The West Point Story" and "Captain Horatio Hornblower."

He is doing marvelously. He really wants to do the right thing. . .During *The Girl from Jones Beach*, Reagan was recently divorced and had lots of girlfriends visiting the set. He was very handsome, as he still is.

Virginia Mayo
People, August 10, 1981

★ ★ .★

I do like Ronnie, I really do. . .My first meeting with him took place at a New Year's Eve party in Los Angeles. His wife, Jane Wyman, had just announced their separation, and it was sad because he did not want a divorce. I remember he went outside. An older woman went with him. He cried. . .He was a very good film actor, he knew his business. . .Nancy was not a very good actress, but she is a beautiful wife to Ronald Reagan.

Patricia Neal
People, August 10, 1981

★ ★ ★

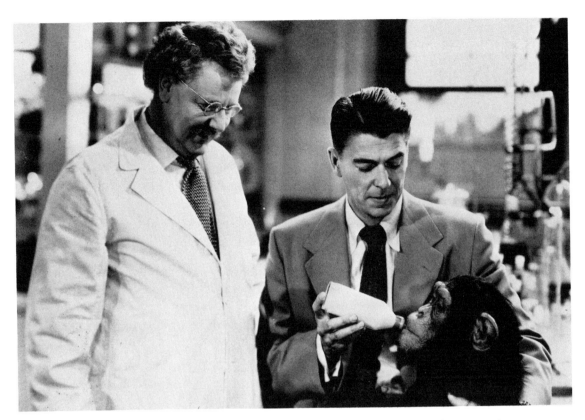

To prove the importance of environment, professor Ronald Reagan took a chimpanzee home to be raised like a human in *Bedtime for Bonzo* (Universal, 1951). Also involved was Walter Slezak.

Milo Anderson was a costume designer at Warner Brothers during Ronald Reagan's years there, and was Jane Wyman's favorite designer.

Ronnie's career was in the doldrums. Big stardom never happened to him, that's why he went further and further into politics.

Milo Anderson
National Enquirer
August 11, 1981

★ ★ ★

Now Mrs. Justin Dart, Jane Bryan appeared with Bette Davis in "The Old Maid" and with Paul Muni in "We Are Not Alone." She appeared with Ronald Reagan in two late-1930s films, "Girls on Probation" and "Brother Rat," and 1940's "Brother Rat and a Baby."

It was always such a pleasure being on the set with Ron Reagan, and I look back upon those years with great joy. He had a wonderful store of marvelous and funny stories and had that great gift of being *so* articulate.

One thing that always interested me was how vitally interested he was in politics. In those days, of course, he was a very, very avid Franklin Roosevelt Democrat and I grew up in a home where my father was a very partisan Republican lawyer.

It was fascinating to me that Ronald Reagan followed the political news as enthusiastically as he followed events in the motion picture industry. His political interest is no new thing but a subject of interest and concern to him as long as I have known him.

Jane Dart (Jane Bryan)
August 11, 1981

★ ★ ★

Herman D. Hover was the owner of Ciro's nightclub in Hollywood.

One night California's Lieutenant Governor at the time, Goodwin Knight, came in while Ronnie and Jane were dining, and Knight made a beeline for Ronnie.

They talked and talked politics, and you could see that Jane was bored. She kept sighing and yawning and making no effort to hide the fact that she thought politics was all very, very dull.

Herman D. Hover
National Enquirer
August 11, 1981

★ ★ ★

Johnny Carson has hosted television's "The Tonight Show Starring Johnny Carson" since 1962. He played cameo roles in the films "Looking for Love" and "Cancel My Reservation."

The Last Outpost (Paramount, 1951) was the first of four films in which Reagan co-starred with redheaded Rhonda Fleming. Happily, all were in color.

Ronald Reagan just signed the new tax law. But I think he was in Hollywood too long. He signed it, "Best wishes, Ronald Reagan."

Johnny Carson
The Tonight Show Starring Johnny Carson (TV)
August 14, 1981

★ ★ ★

Phyllis Thaxter's films include "30 Seconds Over Tokyo," "Bewitched," "Week-end at the Waldorf," "The Sea of Grass," "The Breaking Point," "Come Fill the Cup," "Jim Thorpe—All-American," "Superman" and, with Ronald Reagan in 1952, "She's Working Her Way Through College."

I knew Ronnie only through our work, not socially. He was always fun with a great sense of humor—which he still has. Most intelligent. Looking back, I feel he was a man of integrity, knowledgeable of the problems of our profession and, even at that time, of national affairs.

I starred in the first *General Electric Theater*, live, for CBS: *A Doll's House*, as Nora. Ronnie was their spokesman. There was a party for Mr. Reagan, the G.E. people and the cast given by the CBS heads, Mr. Paley, Dr. Stanton and others. I remember particularly Ronnie's enthusiasm and awareness and thought General Electric was most fortunate in their choice of spokesman. I believe Ronnie had just started to wear contact lenses—he demonstrated how easy they were to handle. I was most impressed and guess the reason I remember so well is that I now wear them myself.

On another G.E. TV show we did together called *The House of Truth*, I recall Nancy coming on the set to visit. I am not sure if they were married then. She was darling, had great style. As a matter of fact, she kept a "loving eye" on him even then. I felt I knew her because her mother had been so kind to me when I was appearing in Chicago in the play *Claudia* in 1941. She talked about Nancy who I believe was at Smith at that time. I also remember my dear friend and fellow MGM player Spencer Tracy telling me that Nancy would be joining us at Metro. Tracy was a good friend of the Davis family and I think he and Mrs. Davis, who had been an actress, had worked together in the theater.

One incident that happened during the filming of *She's Working Her Way Through College* comes to mind. The director, "Lucky" Humberstone, *couldn't stand me*. Either he had someone else in mind for the part and the studio, Warners, insisted on me—or whatever. I was constantly being embarrassed by his remarks on the set. Finally, he went too far and I just plain blew up. Ronnie, who played my husband in the picture, was on the sidelines and said to one of the crew, "Oh, I knew this was going to happen!" He was most sympathetic to both parties and decided the best thing for me to do was leave the set for a while and take a long walk. We toured the Warner lot together until we heard the heads of the studio were on the set and production had been held up over two hours. I remember how understanding and helpful Ronnie was. And thanks to him, I went back on the set with dignity and quietly apologized.

I'd like to add one more thing. While on tour this past year with the play *The Gin Game*, the inevitable question always came up: What was it like working with Ronald Reagan? These questions became more insistent as election time drew near. It gave me the opportunity to give vent to my feelings and admiration for the man.

Ronald Reagan is caught looking more dubious than devoted in this still department pose with Rhonda Fleming for *Hong Kong* (Paramount, 1951).

★ ★ ★

Needless to say, I am delighted he is our President and doing one hell of a job.

Phyllis Thaxter
August 17, 1981

★ ★ ★

Robert Stack has appeared in "First Love," "To Be or Not to Be," "Miss Tatlock's Millions," "A Date with Judy," "Bwana Devil," "Written on the Wind," "1941" and "Airplane!" On TV he starred in "The Untouchables."

I've known Ronald Reagan a long, long time, back in the days when he was president of the Screen Actors Guild. I'll never forget the day he was named president of the union. It was hairy. People were marching atop the roof of the American Legion Stadium. It was a time when hoods were trying to take over the union, and there were threats on Ronnie's life. When I recently saw him, he didn't want to talk about that aspect, but I saw him act well under pressure.

Robert Stack
New York *Daily News*, August 19, 1981

★ ★ ★

James Bacon is a long-time Hollywood reporter and author.

I can remember Ronnie moaning to me in those days—and rightly so—that *She's Working Her Way Through College* and *The Girl from Jones Beach* were the biggest grossing movies the studio, Warner Brothers, made.

"Yet, whenever a good script comes around, they give it to someone like Errol Flynn or Marlon Brando," he said.

I remember saying at the time that perhaps he was in the wrong business. Little did I know what a prophet I was.

James Bacon
Los Angeles Herald Examiner
August 27, 1981

★ ★ ★

Geraldine Fitzgerald, lauded on both stage and screen, has done such films as "Wuthering Heights," "The Gay Sisters," "Watch on the Rhine," "Wilson," "The Strange Affair of Uncle Harry," "Three Strangers," "Ten North Frederick," "Arthur" and, with Ronald Reagan, 1939's "Dark Victory."

When I first went to Hollywood, I went literally from the train to *Dark Victory*, the film in which Ronald Reagan played a sort of beau to Bette Davis, our star. He was, as I recall, very nice-looking, a kind of boy-next-door type, and I was a kind of girl next door who was nevertheless drawn to more menacing, mysterious types. He was more of a brother figure to me.

I remember I wanted to play in what became his great hit, *Kings Row*, in the very dramatic role of Cassie, but Betty Field got the part.

Doris Day and Ronald Reagan were front and center in *The Winning Team* (Warners, 1952), a baseball film which Reagan regards highly. Also pictured, at left: Frank Ferguson.

★ ★ ★

Warner Brothers, where we both worked, was like being on the campus of a very big college, and there were many people there I never even got to meet, let alone know well. After *Dark Victory*, I saw Ronald Reagan around the lot several times but only to say hello. It was the same with Jane Wyman, who would become his wife. I knew her but only to say hello. My memories of Ronald Reagan are of an agreeable and professional colleague.

Thinking back, I felt sorry for him then because he had this "down home" face, as did I, which I thought would keep us from succeeding in more serious things. As it turns out, it was not such a disadvantage to President Reagan after all!

Geraldine Fitzgerald
August 27, 1981

★ ★ ★

Jean-Pierre Aumont's seventy-odd films include "Assignment in Brittany," "The Cross of Lorraine," "Heartbeat," "Lili," "The Seventh Sin," "Hilda Crane," "Day for Night," "The Happy Hooker," "Mahogany" and "Nana."

I met President Reagan at a Hollywood party. It was about 1946. He was interested in politics even then. I told him, "You know, one of these days you are going to end up as President of the United States." And he said, casually, "Yes."

Was Reagan a good actor? Are you kidding? We're going to Washington with our new play—I am not going to say anything about his acting!

Jean-Pierre Aumont
"Last Night with Martin Burden"
New York Post, September 1, 1981

★ ★ ★

President Reagan slept through the Libyan crisis. I understand there are only two reasons you wake up Ronald Reagan. One is World War III. The other is if *Hellcats of the Navy* is on *The Late Show*.

Johnny Carson
The Tonight Show Starring Johnny Carson (TV)
September 1, 1981

★ ★ ★

Nancy Coleman acted with Ronald Reagan in the early 1940s films "Kings Row" and "Desperate Journey." Her other pictures include "Dangerously They Live," "The Gay Sisters," "In Our Time," "Devotion," "Her Sister's Secret" and "Mourning Becomes Electra."

Kings Row was my first movie. I'd just come out to Warner Brothers from the New York stage, but I remember Ronald Reagan being very helpful and kind to me, as if I'd been working there all my life, instead of the new girl in town.

Funny, the things you remember. I was very nearsighted then, and I remember that Mr. Reagan wore contact lenses and showed me how to use them—contact lenses were still quite new.

Reagan had one of his most dramatic roles as troubled baseball great Grover Cleveland Alexander in *The Wining Team* (Warners, 1952). Shown above, from left: Doris Day (whom Reagan dated), Reagan, Dorothy Adams and Kenneth Patterson.

★ ★ ★

People remember us together in the film because of the extreme melodrama unleashed by our characters: I was cast as a girl whose doctor father amputates the legs of her boyfriend (Reagan), perhaps unnecessarily. (That's when Reagan cries "Where's the rest of me?", which became the title of his autobiography.) Actually, I think we really only had one big scene together in the picture. I never really knew him socially. While we were shooting *Kings Row*, I never even *met* Betty Field, who was one of the other stars. We never worked the same day. I didn't meet her until the last day at the cast party!

Only months later came *Desperate Journey*, in which I again shared billing with Ronald Reagan. There was a *group* of young men in this, RAF flyers shot down in Germany; I played a girl there who helped them. Most of my dialogue was with Errol Flynn, so I really recall him better than Mr. Reagan.

I haven't seen Ronald Reagan since the days at Warners, which I left around the mid–1940s. In 1970, however, I taught for ten weeks at the University of California at Davis, which is very near Sacramento, where Reagan was presiding as governor. I thought I might hear from him then, but even though we also did a play there at the time I never did hear.

Nancy Coleman
September 5, 1981

★ ★ ★

Claudette Colbert's illustrious credit list: "Cleopatra," "It Happened One Night," "Imitation of Life," "Arise, My Love," "Remember the Day," "The Palm Beach Story," "So Proudly We Hail," "Since You Went Away," "The Egg and I," "Three Came Home," many more.

No, I never worked with Ronald Reagan. I was older than he was!

Claudette Colbert
New York *Sunday News*
September 6, 1981

★ ★ ★

William Devane has appeared in the television drama "The Missiles of October" plus such theater films as "McCabe and Mrs. Miller," "Family Plot," "Marathon Man," "The Bad News Bears in Breaking Training," "Yanks" and "Honky Tonk Freeway."

President Reagan's doing a good job, isn't he? So much for Alfred Hitchcock's immortal phrase: Actors are just a bunch of cattle.

William Devane
The Merv Griffin Show (TV)
September 8, 1981

★ ★ ★

Impressionist Rich Little has appeared in most fields of entertainment.

The professor and the showgirl: Ronald Reagan cavorts with Virginia Mayo in *She's Working Her Way Through College* (Warners, 1952), musical version of the hardy stage and screen comedy *The Male Animal*.

Right now, I'm very pro-Ronald Reagan. I've met the President and as a matter of fact he did a few impressions for me. He did a Jimmy Stewart impression for me. He was going "Waw. . .Waw. . ." Then an aide interrupted him and said it was time for him to go. And Reagan said, "Would you butt out? Can't you see I'm doing Jimmy Stewart?" Then he did Truman Capote!

Rich Little
Tomorrow Coast-to-Coast Starring Tom Snyder (TV)
September 15, 1981

★ ★ ★

Joanne Woodward's films: "Count Three and Pray," "The Three Faces of Eve," "The Long, Hot Summer," "The Sound and the Fury," "The Fugitive Kind," "From the Terrace," "Rachel, Rachel," "The Effect of Gamma Rays on Man-in-the-Moon Marigolds," etc.

Maybe my husband Paul Newman should run for President. . .not right away. . .become U.S. Senator first. He has the stuff it takes to be President now: he's an actor — a better actor than Ronald Reagan. . .Why would he have to give up auto racing? Reagan didn't give up horseback-riding.

Joanne Woodward
"Last Night with Earl Wilson"
New York Post
September 18, 1981

★ ★ ★

The films of cult favorite Marie Windsor include Gene Kelly's "The Three Musketeers," "Force of Evil," "Hellfire," "The Narrow Margin," "The Sniper," "Trouble Along the Way," "The Killing," "Swamp Women" and "Cahill, United States Marshal."

Many years ago, when Ronnie and Nancy were first married, my husband, Jack Hupp, and I were frequently invited to the home of an old buddy of mine, Audrey Totter, and her husband, Dr. Leo Fred. Since Nancy was also a close friend of Audrey's, Ronnie and Nancy were often at the same dinner parties.

Jack and Ronnie are both great storytellers and the evenings with them were filled with much laughter. Audrey, Nancy and I had been under contract at MGM at the same time and I had known Ronnie somewhat prior to the Nancy-Ronnie merger, so the groupings at the Freds were very congenial, cozy and friendly. Ronnie and Nancy are and always have been warm and affectionate people.

When Ronnie ran for governor, I made several appearances at his rallies and supported him in every way I could. Jack and I contributed to his campaign before he actually declared his intention to run for the Presidency. I have tremendous admiration for him as our President, as a man and as a friend. We have several things in common. We shared the problems of the Screen Actors Guild — I have served on the board of SAG for nineteen years.

By a great coincidence, when Jack and I were married in 1954, we inherited Ronnie's phone number. For years we got calls for him. We still have the same number but we

Reagan was driven to drink by Virginia Mayo in *She's Working Her Way Through College*
(Warners, 1952), although married to Phyllis Thaxter. Film concluded Reagan's fifteen-year
association with Warners.

★ ★ ★

never have to say "wrong number" anymore as the whole world now knows where he can be reached.

Marie Windsor
September, 1981

★ ★ ★

Dame Judith Anderson, star of Broadway's "Medea," has appeared on screen in "Rebecca," "Laura," "And Then There Were None," "Diary of a Chambermaid," "The Strange Love of Martha Ivers," "Pursued," "The Ten Commandments," "Cat on a Hot Tin Roof." In 1942's "Kings Row" she acted with Ronald Reagan.

I am terribly sorry that I cannot be of help to you. I have no recollection of any incidents that occurred during the filming of *Kings Row* with President Reagan. I never saw the film and don't know if I had any scenes with him. (Author's note: she did.) I only recall respect for him as an actor.

Judith Anderson
October, 1981

★ ★ ★

James C. Van Trees, Jr., is the son of cinematographer James Van Trees who photographed Ronald Reagan's first film, "Love is on the Air," as well as Reagan's "Smashing the Money Ring" and "International Squadron."

Dad passed away ten years ago. I was an assistant on the three Ronald Reagan pictures. I remember President Reagan as a very friendly, outgoing young man, interested in everything that went on around the set.

James C. Van Trees, Jr.
October, 1981

★ ★ ★

George Ward is a veteran film agent who handled such stars as Olivia de Havilland, Ann Sheridan, William Powell and Eve Arden. He was Ronald Reagan's first agent in Hollywood.

I had managed Joy Hodges from time to time, and she sent Ronald Reagan to me when I was with the Bill Meiklejohn Agency in Hollywood. Reagan was in California to cover the spring training of the Chicago Cubs in Catalina. When he walked in, I could see that he had something. It was my business to seek out new talent to sell to the studios, and here was a charming, interesting guy with a middle-West freshness.

As I recall, he came into the office on a Thursday and informed me that he was on a limited expense account and was going back to Des Moines radio on Saturday. One of my contacts was Max Arnow, the head of talent at Warner Brothers Studios. I phoned Max and told him I had this attractive, promising young man in the office, and he said, "Bring him out." The studios, you see, were very anxious for new talent then. They sent Ron over to the talent department, where he read for them, and they tested him on Friday. Then he returned to Des Moines.

Ronald Reagan and bride Nancy Davis, left, cut the wedding cake after their marriage on March 4, 1952, in the San Fernando Valley, California. Looking on are William Holden and his actress wife, Brenda Marshall, who attended the ceremony.

On Monday morning, Max Arnow phoned me to say that Jack Warner, head of the studio, had seen the test and they wanted Ron. I reached him with the good news just as he was arriving back in Des Moines. They gave him thirty days, I think, to wrap up his business there. He received a regular seven-year contract, starting at $200 a week. He was probably making $75 a week in Des Moines (actually, pretty good money during the Depression—this was in 1937), so he thought this kind of money was the end of all time.

We became quite close. (We're about the same age—only a few months difference, I think.) He didn't know anyone in Hollywood, so I sort of took him under my wing. I also helped his mother and father get settled when they moved to California, as well as his brother "Moon." Although Bill Meiklejohn often gets the credit for starting Ron in pictures, he didn't even meet him till Ron moved to Hollywood. After a while, Bill sold his business to MCA, which was then in the big band business but anxious to get involved in the film business. All of his contracts automatically went to MCA, too, and so did I. Then Bill left and became head of talent at Paramount Pictures. I stayed with MCA for a while, then went with the Myron Selznick Agency. I couldn't take Reagan with me because he was under contract to MCA.

I saw him quite a bit over the years, though, and I knew his first wife, Jane Wyman, too. I could see the handwriting on the wall where their marriage was concerned. She was an introvert and didn't like to be in the public eye while Ron was always on his soap box about some political issue. There were three actors in Hollywood during those years who were very involved in politics: Adolphe Menjou, George Murphy and Ronald Reagan.

I believe Ron could have developed into a superstar along the lines of a James Stewart, but after a while all he cared about was politics. And the studio bosses resented his stands via the Screen Actors Guild. They said they didn't, but they did.

I saw him when he became governor of California, and have corresponded with him since he became President. He even wrote me from the hospital when he was shot. He has never forgotten the part I played in helping him reach what he is today.

I feel he's an honest, dedicated, grateful man with whose politics, incidentally, I am in accord.

Although I've managed many illustrious people, for some reason I did not bother to save their correspondence. The only two letters I have saved, by some quirk of fate, are from Ronald Reagan, both expressing his happiness and gratitude at being signed by Warner Brothers. They are signed with the nickname by which I've always known him—"Dutch."

George Ward
October 2, 1981

★ ★ ★

Screenwriter Howard Koch's major works: "The Sea Hawk," "Sergeant York," "Casablanca," "Rhapsody in Blue," "Three Strangers" (collaborations); "The Letter," "Mission to Moscow," "Letter from an Unknown Woman," "No Sad Songs for Me" (alone).

I knew Ronald Reagan slightly, just enough to distrust him. We were both members of the Hollywood Democratic Club when liberalism was in fashion (the Roosevelt years). In my memory of meetings we both attended, he was a divisive element and even then a Red-baiter. When a resolution was drawn condemning some atrocity on the part of the Nazis, he would insist on an equal condemnation of the Soviets even though they were our ally in the war against the Nazis. This created a split in the membership that was no doubt a factor in the Club's dissolution.

Rhonda Fleming, Reagan, Estelita and Noah Beery, Jr., traverse the Paramount Pictures lot together between scenes of *Tropic Zone* (1953).

★ ★ ★

I can only conjecture why he moved to the other extreme politically. Possibly as a "B" actor, mostly in "B" pictures, he had a compulsive need for an "A" standing somewhere. He chose politics, made the right connections (right in both senses) and is now getting a fine revenge on those of us who still believe in an egalitarian social order such as existed in the New Deal era and the One World concept of Wilkie and others during the intervening years. In my opinion, Reagan's reign will be short-lived. Will it end with an economic collapse and a popular uprising or with the nuclear war his administration is courting? Being an optimist, I believe we will survive Reagan and the corporate–military oligarchy which he represents.

I can't tell you how Reagan lost the role of Laszlo in *Casablanca* (for which he was announced, before the role went to Paul Henreid), as I came on the screenplay late when the story was pretty much in place and the final cast selected. If Reagan had played the part of a social idealist, I believe the film's popularity would be considerably diminished, perhaps even into black humor in the light of what's happening today.

Howard Koch
October 5, 1981

(Author's note: The original news releases announcing Ronald Reagan's casting in *Casablanca* indicated that he was to be the male star. This means that he was not to have played the secondary role of Laszlo, as generally believed, but the top male character, Rick, immortalized finally by Humphrey Bogart.)

★ ★ ★

Sterling Hayden's films: "Bahama Passage," "The Asphalt Jungle," "So Big," "Johnny Guitar," "The Killing," "The Godfather," "Dr. Strangelove Or: How I Learned to Stop Worrying and Love the Bomb," "Nine to Five," many others.

I have very complicated feelings about him (Ronald Reagan). Along with a lot of people I travel with, it was no, no: he scared us. Now, I see extenuating circumstances. When I was a one-time, would-be Red, I was into social reform. Part of me is still that way. I can understand that the mood of the country, under Reagan, is going stars and stripes again, I can cry when I see the flag. However, to throw in with the conservative right — as I believe the administration is doing — of Chile, El Salvador, Brazil, Argentina or whoever *against the people* — I don't understand this.

He's such a brilliant and articulate man. We saw that back in Hollywood in '51, during the days of the HUAC (House Un-American Activities Committee). But whoever would have dreamed that there would be such a script, that a second- or third-rate actor could make such a transition? No novelist would dare make such a story.

Sterling Hayden
Tomorrow Coast-to-Coast Starring Tom Snyder (TV)
October 6, 1981

★ ★ ★

Bob Hope's many films include seven "Road" pictures plus "The Ghost Breakers," "My Favorite Blonde," "The Princess and the Pirate," "Monsieur Beaucaire," "The Paleface," "Sorrowful Jones," "The Seven Little Foys" and "The Facts of Life."

Two erstwhile Warner Brothers players, Dorothy Malone and Ronald Reagan, were reunited at Universal Studios in *Law and Order* (1953). Neither considers it a career highlight.

Ronnie's hero is Calvin Coolidge and Nancy's is Calvin Klein.

Bob Hope
New York Post
October 19, 1981

★ ★ ★

Gerald Ford was never an actor, but that never stopped some of our Presidents. . .I want to personally welcome President and Mrs. Reagan. He gave up a lot to be here tonight — a rerun of *Knute Rockne* on TV.

Bob Hope
A Bob Hope Celebration
(TV special celebrating the dedication of the
Gerald R. Ford Presidential Museum)
October 22, 1981

★ ★ ★

Ginger Rogers and Fred Astaire were teamed in ten classic movie musicals. On her own, Rogers scored in "Stage Door," "Primrose Path," "Kitty Foyle," "Roxie Hart," "The Major and the Minor," "Lady in the Dark," "I'll Be Seeing You," "Week-end at the Waldorf" and opposite Ronald Reagan, the 1951 release "Storm Warning."

In 1950 he (Reagan) and I co-starred in a film called *Storm Warning*, and I found then that he always gives everything he has to what he's doing.

Last March I was a guest at the Gridiron Club dinner in Washington. President Reagan was the last speaker. During his speech he looked at me on the dais and said:

"Ginger Rogers, I'm glad you're here tonight. You and I appeared in the film *Storm Warning*, but I was never really sure what the title meant until I met Tip O'Neill."

I've always thought he was very good at whatever he did. He brought great honesty and integrity to his performances.

Ginger Rogers
Play House Quintessence Series
Cleveland, Ohio
October 26, 1981

(Thomas P. "Tip" O'Neill, Jr., a Democrat, is speaker of the House of Representatives and leader of the opposition to most of Reagan's legislative programs.)

★ ★ ★

Vernon Scott has been reporting on the Hollywood scene for many years.

Jane Wyman is one of a kind, the first and only ex-wife of a sitting President of the United States.

In the two hundred years of the republic, no other woman has held that unique position, because Ronald W. Reagan is the first divorced man to win the Presidency.

Therefore, Jane Wyman, an Academy Award-winning actress, to be sure, will become a footnote in history long after her screen performances and her acting contemporaries are forgotten.

Reagan and Steve Forrest had the major roles in *Prisoner of War* (MGM, 1954), a story of mistreated American captives during the Korean war.

★ ★ ★

Wyman, 67, has scrupulously refrained from commenting on her former husband before and since his election. She said virtually nothing about Reagan during his eight-year tenure as California governor.

Vernon Scott
Los Angeles Daily News
November 4, 1981

★ ★ ★

Recording/nightclub star Connie Francis appeared in such films as "Where the Boys Are," "Follow the Boys," "Looking for Love" and "Where the Boys Meet the Girls."

(Re her appointment to a Presidential crime commission:)
I'm Ronnie Reagan's biggest fan. I send him two or three letters a week. I write and say, "What did you do for us today?". . .I wrote him and said, "My biggest claim to fame is that I'm the world's best known crime victim. . .I want to help". . .So, in addition to working with crime victims now, I want to get new laws.

No, I don't want to be a politician, I'm too honest for that—*except for Ronnie, except for Ronnie!!*

Connie Francis
Good Morning New York (TV)
November 5, 1981

★ ★ ★

Olivia de Havilland has starred in a number of movie classics, including "The Adventures of Robin Hood," "Gone with the Wind," "Hold Back the Dawn," "Princess O'Rourke," "To Each His Own," "The Dark Mirror," "The Snake Pit" and "The Heiress." In 1940, she acted with Ronald Reagan in "Santa Fe Trail."

As to recollections of Ronald Reagan, what comes most to mind is his affability and his gift for conducting Screen Actors Guild meetings with adroitness and good humor. I think he was always an instinctive politician, and a genial one.

Olivia de Havilland
November 6, 1981

★ ★ ★

Producer and artist's manager Allan Carr has been involved with "Survive," "Grease," "Tommy," "The Deer Hunter," "Can't Stop the Music" and "Grease 2."

I thought the White House should have the best. They had this old screen and projector. I put in a new CinemaScope screen and stereophonic sound, Dolby Stereo. . .I paid retail. Just last week I got this letter from Ronald Reagan. He wasn't in office when I fixed up the

Reagan visited MGM, the Tiffany's of Hollywood, to make *Prisoner of War* (1954), far from the glossy entertainments for which the lot was known. Pictured: Steve Forrest, Reagan, Dewey Martin, Robert Horton and Darryl Hickman.

screening room, but he wrote, "Thank you. Now my wife and I get to watch movies. . ." I ran off xeroxes of it for my friends.

Allan Carr
Tomorrow Coast-to-Coast Starring Tom Snyder (TV), 1981

★　★　★

Notable among Rhonda Fleming's more than forty films are "Spellbound," "The Spiral Staircase," "A Connecticut Yankee in King Arthur's Court," "Gunfight at the O.K. Corral" and four co-starring with Ronald Reagan: 1951's "The Last Outpost" and "Hong Kong," 1953's "Tropic Zone" and 1955's "Tennessee's Partner."

For some reason, I can't tell you too much about Ronald Reagan from the films we made together. I guess I was too busy just doing my job. I do remember that he used to hold court between scenes with the crew and expound on, I presume, politics. I can't tell you exactly what he was saying, because I was always too busy rushing off to get into my next costume or whatever to listen.

Rhonda Fleming
November 15, 1981

★　★　★

Marguerite Chapman was a popular leading lady in such films as "Appointment in Berlin," "Destroyer," "My Kingdom for a Cook," "Counter-Attack," "Pardon My Past," "Mr. District Attorney," "Relentless," "Coroner Creek" and "The Gallant Blade."

In 1941 I was still new in films and was under contract to Warner Brothers. There were six of us who made up the Navy Blues Sextette in the Ann Sheridan picture called *Navy Blues*. At the time, I was sharing a house with one of the other gals in the Sextette, Peggy Diggins.

Peggy and I also appeared with Ronald Reagan's then-wife, Jane Wyman, in *You're in the Army Now* and *The Body Disappears*.

One day we went to lunch at the Warner Brothers commissary, and all of a sudden I realized I somehow had gotten seated at the wrong table, right across from Ronald Reagan and a couple of others. I called over to Peggy to make sure we were going to mass on Sunday or communion or whatever.

Reagan picked up on this and said to me, "Are you a Catholic?"

I said, "Yes."

He said, "Why?"

I said, "I was *born* one."

He went on, "That doesn't mean you have to stay one."

Now it just so happened that I had done considerable research into various religions to make sure of the one I wanted. He continued to put me on about it and embarrassed me in front of everyone. He was a big shot at Warners then, was probably shooting *Kings Row*, but I was no small potatoes myself: I had been a top model in New York. I never liked him since then. I noticed that there was never any mention of religion in his career until he became President, and then there was some publicity about Nancy and him going to a Protestant church. I voted for him, though—there wasn't much else to choose from! At least he has the guts to follow his beliefs.

One he'd like to forget: *Cattle Queen of Montana* (RKO, 1954). Reagan enjoyed working with legendary Hollywood star Barbara Stanwyck and Rodd Redwing, but the film's virtues stop there.

Of course, a Robin Hood he ain't — a hooded robin, maybe.

Marguerite Chapman
November 18, 1981

★ ★ ★

Howard Duff's films include "Brute Force," "The Naked City," "All My Sons," "Calamity Jane and Sam Bass," "Woman in Hiding," "Private Hell 36," "A Wedding" and "Kramer Vs. Kramer." He starred in the television series "Flamingo Road."

Our President says there was no blacklist, so I guess mine didn't happen. At the time, my name appeared with many other alleged Communist sympathizers in a magazine *(Red Channels)*. We all laughed when we read it. But as it turned out, I couldn't get on a TV show for two years.

Howard Duff
The John Davidson Show (TV)
November 19, 1981

★ ★ ★

Jane Wilkie was a Hollywood fan magazine writer who later wrote the books "Confessions of an Ex-Fan Magazine Writer" and, collaborating with Nancy Reagan, "To Love a Child."

Other than his shocking timing when he asked June Allyson to tell him all about Dick Powell's illness and death (the day after Powell's passing), I remember him in the Reagan home in the days when he was married to Jane Wyman. I was interviewing Jane when "Ronnie" hove to and, as he polished his riding boots, held forth without a pause on a political diatribe. It struck me that Jane was faintly bored by the lecturer.

Jane Wilkie
Confessions of an Ex-Fan Magazine Writer
by Jane Wilkie
Doubleday Publishers, 1981

★ ★ ★

Lester Cole, one of the "Hollywood 10" jailed in 1950, wrote or co-wrote the screenplays for "The House of the Seven Gables," "Among the Living," "Objective Burma," "Blood on the Moon," "The Romance of Rosy Ridge" and (pseudonymously) "Born Free."

We found supporters (against the House Un-American Activities Committee) in a quickly formed group of some of the most famous actors, writers and directors calling themselves The Committee for the First Amendment. . .I failed then to notice the conspicuous absence of such self-proclaimed liberals as — Ronald Reagan.
. . .The Committee on the Arts, Sciences and Professions (A.S.P.) sent me to Ronnie Reagan's (then pronounced R*ee*gan) house to ask him to a meeting of the First Amendment group. It was early evening when I arrived and Jane Wyman, then his wife, came to the door. Wyman told me Reagan was lying down, not feeling well, but she'd talk to him.

Reagan, who was a good horseman, had fun doing such Westerns as *Cattle Queen of Montana* (RKO, 1954). He didn't have the title role—that was Barbara Stanwyck.

★ ★ ★

She was back in moments, seemingly embarrassed, and asked me to tell Humphrey Bogart and Willie Wyler that he was not well, but was thinking seriously about joining them. He would let them know the next day.

He didn't. His career from then on swung more and more to the right.

Lester Cole
Hollywood Red, by Lester Cole
Ramparts Press Publishers, 1981

★ ★ ★

It's nice that Reagan tells jokes instead of appointing them.

Bob Hope
"The Great Life," by George Christy
The Hollywood Reporter
November 19, 1981

★ ★ ★

I think it's fine (Reagan becoming President). I think it's a step forward for actors. I think President Reagan thinks so, too. . .I don't talk fast enough to be a politician.

James Stewart
Entertainment Tonight (TV)
November 20, 1981

★ ★ ★

Alan King has appeared in "Miracle in the Rain," "The Helen Morgan Story," "Bye Bye Braverman," "The Anderson Tapes," "Just Tell Me What You Want" and "Author! Author!"

Reagan keeps winning one for "the Gipper." He thinks the world is one big Western.

Alan King
Asbury Park Press
November 22, 1981

★ ★ ★

Rona Barrett is a multi-media journalist covering the entertainment industry.

President Reagan is a master with the media.

Rona Barrett
The John Davidson Show (TV)
November 25, 1981

★ ★ ★

Reagan's final big screen appearance with Rhonda Fleming was in the Bret Harte story, *Tennessee's Partner* (RKO, 1955). The trio above, from left, consists of John Payne, Fleming and Reagan.

★ ★ ★

Pat O'Brien did three movies with Ronald Reagan: 1938's "The Cowboy from Brooklyn" and "Boy Meets Girl" and 1940's "Knute Rockne, All American." He also appeared in "The Front Page," "Angels with Dirty Faces," "The Fighting 69th," "Torrid Zone," "Some Like It Hot" and "Ragtime."

Ron's dad and myself have been known to toast a friend and we made many friends the evening that we met. . .Early this year Ron and I received Honorary Doctorate degrees at Knute Rockne's Notre Dame University. There was quite an ovation, and while we were embracing Ron whispered in my ear, "I guess they liked the picture."

Pat O'Brien
Ronald Reagan: At Home on the Ranch
with Barbara Walters (TV)
November 26, 1981

★ ★ ★

We'd sit around at lunch (during the filming of *Storm Warning)* and Ronnie would talk—guess what?—politics. He talked politics for the whole hour at every lunchtime.

Ginger Rogers
Ronald Reagan: At Home on the Ranch
with Barbara Walters (TV)
November 26, 1981

★ ★ ★

Earl Hamner is creator of the TV series "The Waltons" and the 1981 comeback series for Jane Wyman, "Falcon Crest."

I feel Jane Wyman is a celebrity in her own right. She is one of the legendary stars. She is a great actress. If anybody asks her any questions about Mr. Reagan while I'm there, I try to deflect them. . .We have not attempted to capitalize on the relationship in any way.

Earl Hamner
"Jane Wyman: 'I Always Did Four-Handkerchief Roles. Until Now.' "
by Marianne Costantinou
The New York Times, November 29, 1981

★ ★ ★

Henry Fonda's dozens of films include "Young Mr. Lincoln," "The Grapes of Wrath," "The Lady Eve," "The Male Animal," "The Big Street," "The Ox-Bow Incident," "Fort Apache," "Mister Roberts," "12 Angry Men" and "On Golden Pond."

Reagan is a major concern. I think we're headed for disaster. I'm surprised there isn't more opposition. He upsets me so it's hard to talk about. How did he get elected? He's a hell of a speech-maker. He says the things people want to hear. He says them very convincingly and with what sounds like sincerity and he's talking a language that people

Ronald Reagan and Nancy Davis (Reagan) in their only film together, *Hellcats of the Navy* (Columbia, 1957), a true story of World War II. Reagan played a naval officer, Nancy a nurse.

haven't heard for a long time and it impresses them. *I listen to a Reagan speech and want to throw up!*

Henry Fonda
"Playboy Interview"
Playboy, December, 1981

★　★　★

Jane Fonda's films: "Cat Ballou," "Barbarella," "They Shoot Horses, Don't They?", "Klute," "Julia," "Coming Home," "The China Syndrome," "Nine to Five," "On Golden Pond," more.

There is a reason why Israel is solarized to the extent that it is.
Virtually every rooftop in Japan has a collector.
We're nowhere. Reagan has not even mentioned conservation.

Jane Fonda
"When Jane Fonda Speaks, Does the Press Listen?"
by James Verniere
The Aquarian, December 8-16, 1981

★　★　★

Warren Beatty's major films: "Splendor in the Grass," "The Roman Spring of Mrs. Stone," "All Fall Down," "Bonnie and Clyde," "Shampoo," "Heaven Can Wait" and "Reds."

How can you not like him (Reagan) when he remembers conversations that took place fifteen years ago?

Warren Beatty
New York Post
December 10, 1981

★　★　★

Child actor Ricky Schroder has played leads in "The Champ," "The Last Flight of Noah's Ark" and "The Earthling," as well as the TV movie "Little Lord Fauntleroy." He starred in the television series "Silver Spoons."

We went to the White House for the American Lung Association—I'm the youth ambassador. We went in the Oval Office with President Reagan. We met him for about twenty-five minutes. He and Mrs. Reagan were such warm people. He gave me a jar of jelly beans. He told us he was talking to a world leader once and the world leader said, "Oh! Can I have some jelly beans?" They don't have candy in some countries, you know. It was pretty funny. I got an autograph. I was really nervous, but I said, "Mr. President, may I have your autograph?" He wrote, "To Ricky. With warm regards, Ronald Reagan."

In March 1962, Jeanne Crain and Reagan co-starred in the final presentation of *The General Electric Theater* entitled *My Dark Days*. He had been with the GE television program as spokesman, host and sometimes star for the series' eight-year existence.

★ ★ ★

We have it framed in our hallway.

Ricky Schroder
The Merv Griffin Show (TV)
December 14, 1981

★ ★ ★

I only know Ronnie from that one film that we did *(Night unto Night)*, and he was distant. He presented an image just like he does today. He has not changed.

I suppose that is why he was never really a great actor, because he never took that mask off.

I was really hot on Don Siegel, who directed the film, and that's where my eyes were.

Viveca Lindfors
"Box Seat: Viva Viveca!", by Danielle Roter
The Los Angeles Herald Examiner
December 17, 1981

★ ★ ★

Noah Beery's long career has been highlighted by such films as "Only Angels Have Wings," "Of Mice and Men," "Sergeant York," "Gung Ho!", "The Story of Will Rogers," "The Best Little Whorehouse in Texas" and, with Ronald Reagan, 1951's "The Last Outpost" and 1953's "Tropic Zone." On TV he co-starred in "The Rockford Files."

When Noah Beery was apprised that both he and Ronald Reagan had been among those actors once talked about for the title role in the film biography of Will Rogers (eventually played by Will Rogers, Jr.), Beery replied:

I remember many people being up for Will Rogers, but not the Prez.

As for our professional relationship, he was always fun to work with and a fine horseman.

Noah Beery
December 20, 1981

★ ★ ★

Lee Bonnell, the husband-manager of Gale Storm, acted in several films, including "Parachute Battalion," "Lady Scarface," "Look Who's Laughing," "Army Surgeon" and "The Navy Comes Through."

For a time I tried to get into the production end of the movie business with religious subjects. I was inspired by the story of Bill Alexander, a minister from Oklahoma who came to Hollywood to give a talk and had them in the aisles cheering. Ronald Reagan, who was president of the Screen Actors Guild at that time and belonged to our church, was to follow. I remember saying, "Ronnie, Bill's a tough act to follow." Ronnie smiled and said,

Reagan made his last feature film appearance portraying a villain in *The Killers* (Universal, 1964). It was a remake of the 1946 film adapted from Ernest Hemingway's short story.

"I'll do my best." He had them cheering, too. I never underestimated him after that.

Lee Bonnell
I Ain't Down Yet, by Gale Storm with Bill Libby
Bobbs–Merrill Publishers, 1981

★　★　★

Comedian David Steinberg has appeared in the films "The End" and "Something Short of Paradise." He directed "Paternity."

1981, the year that brought together for the first time Nixon, Ford, Carter and Reagan—a Mt. Rushmore of incompetence.

David Steinberg
The Tonight Show Starring Johnny Carson (TV)
January 5, 1982

★　★　★

Alan Alda, star of the long-running TV series "M*A*S*H", has appeared in the films "Gone Are the Days," "Paper Lion," "The Mephisto Waltz," "The Moonshine Wars," "The Seduction of Joe Tynan" and "The Four Seasons."

I love people's ordinariness. . .I don't think there are heroes. I think there are ordinary people who behave heroically at times. Therefore, everybody is capable of being heroic. I don't know about any famous heroes that I can get a handle on because they don't seem real to me. Take Reagan. The public persona that he presents is of a likeable person. But that's not saying much because that doesn't mean that you're talking about a *real* person.

Alan Alda
"In Search of Alan Alda," by Timothy White
Attenzione, January, 1982

★　★　★

Ava Gardner's films: "The Killers," "One Touch of Venus," "Show Boat," "Pandora and the Flying Dutchman," "The Snows of Kilimanjaro," "Mogambo," "The Barefoot Contessa," "The Sun Also Rises," "Night of the Iguana," others.

Reagan's performance as President of the United States?
No better than his acting.

Ava Gardner
People, January 11, 1982

★　★　★

Mort Sahl is a socially conscious comedian-actor who has been featured in such films as "In Love and War," "All the Young Men," "Johnny Cool," "Doctor, You've Got to Be Kidding" and "Don't Make Waves."

California Governor-elect Ronald Reagan, wife Nancy and children Patti and Ronald hang a Christmas wreath at their Pacific Palisades home in December, 1966.

★ ★ ★

I was at dinner with him (Reagan) recently. We're close friends. I'm *very* close to Mrs. Reagan—we've been friends for years.

He's always picking up eighty-year-old Social Security recipients out of wheelchairs and saying, "When I was your age I was working."

Mort Sahl
Midday with Bill Boggs (TV)
January 22, 1982

★ ★ ★

Lana Turner's major movies: "Ziegfeld Girl," "Honky Tonk," "Johnny Eager," "The Postman Always Rings Twice," "Green Dolphin Street," "Cass Timberlane," "The Three Musketeers," "The Bad and the Beautiful," "Peyton Place," "Imitation of Life."

I really don't remember anything about him (Reagan). . .It's funny, people tell me we used to date.

Even my mother keeps insisting we went out a few times. But believe me, I never dated him. . .Those photos of us were taken all in one day at the Warner Brothers ranch.

Lana Turner
"Lana Turner: I Never Dated Ronald Reagan"
by Jeanne Jakle
The San Antonio News, February 3, 1982

(In his autobiography, Ronald Reagan said that when he and Lana Turner were both newcomers under contract to Warner Brothers in the late 1930s, he escorted her to a premiere—not in the usual limousine, but in a taxi.)

★ ★ ★

Lee Remick's films: "A Face in the Crowd," "Wild River," "The Long, Hot Summer," "Anatomy of a Murder," "The Days of Wine and Roses," "No Way to Treat a Lady," "Sometimes a Great Notion," "A Severed Head," "The Omen," etc.

I'm inclined for the most part to agree with Reagan (that movies were better "when the actors kept their clothes on"). Then ideas become. . .stronger, and movies more fun to watch in the long run. Bodies are pretty much the same. Whereas to be moved emotionally, to laugh, that's special, that's golden.

Lee Remick
The Merv Show (TV)
February 5, 1982

★ ★ ★

Dewey Martin appeared with Ronald Reagan in 1954's "Prisoner of War," and also was in "The Thing," "Battleground," "The Big Sky," "Tennessee Champ," "Men of the Fighting Lady," "The Desperate Hours," "Land of the Pharaohs" and "The Proud and the Profane."

Nancy Reagan watches husband Ronald take the oath of office as the thirty-third Governor
of California on January 2, 1967.

I did that *(Prisoner of War)* with Ronald Reagan, and it was a fairly good little film. Ronnie was always professional and a perfect gentleman; he had a lot of class. The film was double-billed but a pleasure to make and the (MGM) contractees were all great guys. Let's see: Robert Horton, Steve Forrest, hard to remember them all.

Dewey Martin
"Catching Up with Dewey Martin," by Jeff Parker
Hollywood Studio Magazine, Februray, 1982

★　★　★

Among Lily Tomlin's films: "Nashville," "The Late Show," "Moment by Moment," "Nine to Five" and "The Incredible Shrinking Woman."

If we could attract enough attention, create enough focus (on the nuclear weapon problem) — so that Brezhnev and Reagan would sit down and talk. They aren't even *talking* anymore!
If they would just stop manufacturing weapons *now*. . .
There's lot of propaganda in the media that we could win a nuclear war. What kind of mind even *thinks* about winning a nuclear war?

Lily Tomlin
The Merv Show (TV)
February 10, 1982

★　★　★

Lena Horne's films: "Cabin in the Sky," "Stormy Weather," "Broadway Rhythm," "Ziegfeld Follies," "Till the Clouds Roll By," "Words and Music." She capped her career with "Lena Horne: The Lady and Her Music" on Broadway.

After discussing the male film stars who to her had the most sex appeal, Lena Horne was asked if she saw President Reagan as "a romantic figure." She replied only:
For heaven's sake!

Lena Horne
"The Lady is a Champ," by Bernard Gavzer
Parade, February 7, 1982

★　★　★

Screen Actors Guild President Ed Asner, on TV many years with his portrayal of newsman Lou Grant, has acted in such films as "El Dorado," "Change of Habit," "The Call Me MR. Tibbs," "Skin Game," "Fort Apache, The Bronx" and "Daniel."

We have called this press conference for two purposes: The first is to announce to the nation that an organization called "Medical Aid to El Salvador" has been established. . .to raise money in the United States to support the health care system of the Democratic Revolutionary Front in El Salvador. . .
Our second purpose is to announce that we, and many of our colleagues in the entertainment industry, intend to play an increasingly active role in support of Medical Aid for El Salvador. . .

Ronald Reagan in 1968.

★ ★ ★

Yet while those of us here pledge ourselves to send medical supplies to the one side in this war committed to delivering them to the people in need, we find our government sending machine guns and helicopter gunships to the other side. Today we want to say clearly to President Reagan in the White House and Secretary Haig in the State Department that their enemies in El Salvador are not our enemies.

Ed Asner
Washington, D.C.
February 15, 1982

★ ★ ★

When TV talk show host Merv Griffin interrupted guest Jane Fonda to ask if she was saying that an actor shouldn't run for high political office, she replied:

That's absolutely right. I think that Ronald Reagan is wonderful on television, he's a good person. I know his daughter Patti. He's a good guy, a good father. He's very good on television. But these are not necessarily the qualities that will get us out of this quagmire we're in.

. . .When he grew up, when he was young, it was Mom and Pop stores. . .a less complex world. That was the beginning of the 1900s. Now it's more complicated, it doesn't work.

Jane Fonda
The Merv Show (TV)
February 15, 1982

★ ★ ★

Eve Arden's numerous films include "Ziegfeld Girl," "Cover Girl," "Mildred Pierce," "Night and Day," "One Touch of Venus," "Our Miss Brooks," "Anatomy of a Murder," "Grease," "Grease 2" and, with Ronald Reagan, 1947's "The Voice of the Turtle."

It's a little difficult to judge his (Reagan's) accomplishments as President. I'm a little concerned about all the budget cuts. That disturbs me.

I can't understand how, out of that, can come the good that he expects.

Eve Arden
National Enquirer
February 16, 1982

★ ★ ★

Ruth Hussey's films include "Northwest Passage," "The Philadelphia Story," "Flight Command," "Tennessee Johnson," "The Uninvited," "The Great Gatsby," "The Lady Wants Mink," "The Facts of Life" and, co-starring with Ronald Reagan, 1950's "Louisa."

I'd say he (Reagan) is first-rate. His cutting down on spending in the face of so much opposition means that he's very courageous. He's kept his campaign promises.

Senator George Murphy and Governor of California Ronald Reagan in 1968. They are old friends and co-starred in *This is the Army* (Warners, 1943).

He stood up to Congress and has done what he thinks is right for the country.

Ruth Hussey
National Enquirer
February 16, 1982

★ ★ ★

I would rate Ron very highly as President. He's done some things that are very unpopular. He's stopped the giveaway programs. We needed to do that. He's one of the most courageous Presidents we've ever had.

Virginia Mayo
National Enquirer
February 16, 1982

★ ★ ★

Eleanor Parker has given fine performances in "Pride of the Marines," "Caged," "Detective Story," "Scaramouche," "Interrupted Melody," "The Man with the Golden Arm," "Home from the Hill," "The Sound of Music" and opposite Ronald Reagan, 1947's "The Voice of the Turtle."

I think Reagan's doing great. I think he's doing just fine.
I hope everything goes great for him.

Eleanor Parker
National Enquirer
February 16, 1982

★ ★ ★

I certainly would rate him (Reagan) up there with some of our top presidents. He is to this age what Lincoln was to his age.

Ginger Rogers
National Enquirer
February 16, 1982

★ ★ ★

Efrem Zimbalist, Jr., has acted frequently on TV, as well as in the films "House of Strangers," "Band of Angels," "Too Much, Too Soon," "Home Before Dark," "By Love Possessed," "The Chapman Report" and "Wait until Dark."

I campaigned for Reagan in 1976, and I was a delegate to the Republican convention. I worked for him again in 1980, but I wasn't a delegate. And we both worked for Barry

Author Doug McClelland, left, as editor of *Record World* magazine, meets First Daughter Maureen Reagan, circa 1970. Maureen was then hoping for a singing career and stopped by with her current recording. Pictured, too, are the magazine's associate editor, David Finkle, and record company man Don Miller.

Goldwater in 1964, although he certainly did more than I.

Efrem Zimbalist, Jr.
Asbury Park Press
February 20, 1982

★ ★ ★

In a long screen career, Dana Andrews has appeared in "Tobacco Road," "The Ox-Bow Incident," "The Purple Heart," "Laura," "State Fair," "A Walk in the Sun," "The Best Years of Our Lives," "Boomerang" and "My Foolish Heart."

Thirty years ago at lunch, Ronald Reagan, William Holden and I ordered drinks and some food, and a little later the waiter asked if we wanted another drink. Holden and I answered, sure, we'd have another. Reagan turned to us and said, "What do you want another drink for? You just had one." Well, that was the difference between a probable alcoholic (Andrews), a possible alcoholic (Holden) and a man who, no way, would ever become an alcoholic.

Dana Andrews
New York *Sunday News*
February 21, 1982

★ ★ ★

Pat Boone's films: "Bernardine," "April Love," "Mardi Gras," "Journey to the Center of the Earth," "State Fair," "Goodbye, Charlie" and "The Greatest Story Ever Told."

When Reagan first sought support to run for Governor of California, everybody in show business seemed to be a Democrat. The only ones (besides me) for Reagan were Victor Jory, Wendell Corey and Piper Laurie. After a while, John Wayne and Roy and Dale Rogers came in. Then, a year later, Sinatra, Dean Martin and a few more.
What you see is what you get. There is no artifice about Reagan, no game-playing.

Pat Boone
New York *Sunday News*
February 21, 1982

★ ★ ★

I just happen to think that fella's (Reagan) doing a hell of a job.

James Stewart
New York *Sunday News*
February 21, 1982

★ ★ ★

Jack Lemmon's films: "Mister Roberts," "My Sister Eileen," "Some Like It Hot," "The Apartment," "The Days of Wine and Roses," "The Odd Couple," "Save the Tiger," "The China Syndrome," "Missing," etc.

Governor Ronald Reagan toasts his one-time boss, movie mogul Jack L. Warner, right, at a 1973 testimonial dinner held on Warner Brothers' vast Stage 1, converted into a ballroom for the occasion. Frank Sinatra emceed.

Reagan gave us a tour of their private quarters in the White House and showed me some of his gym equipment—and, with his coat on, demonstrated some of it. He's in great shape! He was so charming that although I am a long-time Democrat, I might vote for him!

Jack Lemmon
"Just for Variety," by Army Archerd
Daily Variety, February 23, 1982

★ ★ ★

Reagan was a little upset with Ed Asner (and his speech against U.S. policy in El Salvador). He said, "What does an actor know about politics?"

Johnny Carson
The Tonight Show Starring Johnny Carson (TV)
February 25, 1982

★ ★ ★

I'm not surprised that miniskirts are coming back. They've proved the same thing as Reaganomics: that less is better. . .The President has inspired a new drink called the Federalism. You drink it in Washington and charge it to the people back home.

Bob Hope
Bob Hope's Women I Love—Beautiful and Funny (TV)
February 28, 1982

★ ★ ★

Michael Caine's films: "Zulu," "Alfie," "The Ipcress File," "Gambit," "Sleuth," "The Man Who Would Be King," "California Suite," "Dressed to Kill" and "Deathtrap."

I'm a Cockney. . .In England, the lower classes speak quickly to get people's attention, while the uppercrust speaks slowly with many pauses, knowing that people are hanging on their every word. You will notice that the more powerful people are, the more slowly they speak. You'll notice Ronald Reagan says "Welll" and then goes on from there.

Michael Caine
The Tonight Show Starring Johnny Carson (TV)
March 4, 1982

★ ★ ★

I went to Jack Warner and said there was a young man on the lot that I've been watching. I said he throws the football around pretty well, and I said I don't know whom you are considering (for the role of football star George Gipp in *Knute Rockne, All American*), but a lot of people are in the pack for consideration who don't know a football from a watermelon—this guy does! Plus, he can act. So that was it, Ronnie got the part, and we've been close friends ever since. In fact, recently Ron and I received Honorary Doctorate

To Doug McClelland
With best wishes,

Ronald Reagan

President Ronald Reagan autographed this photo for the author in 1981.

★ ★ ★

degrees at Notre Dame. He just sent me a picture of that occasion, signed RON. That's class.

Pat O'Brien
"Pat O'Brien: Reunited with Cagney After Twenty Years"
by Bill Kelly
Hollywood Studio Magazine, March, 1982

★ ★ ★

There is a power struggle going on between President Reagan's advisors. Moe and Curley are out. Larry is still in.

Johnny Carson
The Tonight Show Starring Johnny Carson (TV)
March 4, 1982

★ ★ ★

Can you imagine? All this and Ronnie is President!

Claudette Colbert

(As she embraced her contemporary screen great Bette Davis at the American Film Institute Tribute to director Frank Capra on March 4, 1982.)

Reported by Liz Smith, *Live at Five* (TV)
March 8, 1982

★ ★ ★

The good news is President Reagan said today he can see the economic light at the end of the tunnel. The bad news is it's a guy with a flashlight looking for food. . .President Reagan and Nancy celebrated their thirtieth anniversary today at their ranch in Santa Barbara walking by their pond. They're going to release a film of it called *On Golden Pond II*.

Johnny Carson
The Tonight Show Starring Johnny Carson (TV)
March 5, 1982

★ ★ ★

John Davidson, star of TV's "That's Incredible!" and his own talk-variety series, has appeared in the films "The Happiest Millionaire," "The One and Only Genuine Original Family Band" and "The Concorde. . .Airport '79."

As our leader, I think he's (Reagan) done a wonderful job.

John Davidson
The John Davidson Show (TV)
March 11, 1982

At the White House in 1981, Ronald and Nancy Reagan greet members of the Presidential Inaugural Committee and others, including (to the left of the President) Ginger Rogers, a supporter and former co-star of the President.

Missing wasn't screened for him (President Reagan). He stole it. They were supposed to have a press screening that night at the American Film Institute in Washington, and all of a sudden they said, "We're not having one tonight." He took the only print and ran it at Camp David (on February 10, two days after the State Department released its three-page rebuttal to the politically controversial film).

Then, two nights later, my wife, Felicia, and I and some friends were invited to the White House. Now, I would never have asked the President what he thought of the film because it would have put him in a terribly awkward position. The State Department had taken a stand, and he can't refute that to me.

So we're sitting there at the dinner table, and after about an hour or so, Jim Mahoney, my press agent, said to the President, "Did you see the picture?" Of course, we all knew that he had.

All he said, after he took a sip of wine, was "Yes, I've seen it," and smiled. And we all laughed. Then Nancy said, "I thought Jack was wonderful, but obviously we wish it had been more upbeat." And I thought, "More upbeat?!"

Jack Lemmon
"Another Controversy for Films' Nonaggressive Good Guy"
by Larry Kart
Chicago Tribune, March 14, 1982

★ ★ ★

Mickey Rooney's lifetime in show business has included ten films with Judy Garland, the Hardy Family series and "Boys Town," "Young Tom Edison," "The Human Comedy," "National Velvet," "Summer Holiday," "Words and Music" and "Killer McCoy." On Broadway: "Sugar Babies."

I just cried when my great friend Ron Reagan got elected President. And now his critics are starting to devour him, you say. Well, that's all right. . .because he devours *them*. The moment the wolves start baying and the dikes start breaking, this man. . .thrives.

Mickey Rooney
"The Battling Bantam of Broadway"
by Paul Hendrickson
The Washington Post, March 14, 1982

★ ★ ★

Barbara Billingsley, the mother on television's "Leave It to Beaver," appeared with Ronald Reagan in 1950s TV and has the distinction of having worked in films with both Reagan wives: Jane Wyman in "Three Guys Named Mike" and Nancy Davis in "Shadow on the Wall." Other features: "The Bad and the Beautiful," "The Tall Target," "Airplane!", etc.

I worked opposite President Reagan in two *Schlitz Playhouse of Stars* television shows in the early 1950s, and I enjoyed him very much. I even campaigned for him when he was running for Governor of California. I've heard him speak many times, but met him only once since we worked together. That was in Kansas City when he was successfully running for the Presidency.

Child actor Ricky Schroder, American Lung Association youth ambassador, presents President and Mrs. Ronald Reagan with a sheet of Christmas seals in a White House ceremony in 1981.

★ ★ ★

He's charming, kind, honest, intelligent and wants the best for our country. And he's certainly not against "the little man," never has been, nor is he bigoted in any way. I liked him, still do and so did my late husband.

One evening a while back, I talked to the President's daughter, Maureen Reagan, for a long time, and their family life when she was a child certainly sounded normal and happy, as she described it.

I was under contract to MGM when Nancy Davis was there, but knew her only slightly, although I did appear in what she says was her first movie, *Shadow on the Wall*.

Barbara Billingsley
March 16, 1982

★ ★ ★

Ever since Reagan was host for *G.E. Theater*, these very, very right-wing people have taken care of him. The Reagans were always the poorest people in the richest crowd.

"A Hollywood Producer"
"Really Cheap Chic," by Carol Troy
The Village Voice, March 16, 1982

★ ★ ★

Frank Coghlan, who began acting as a child in silent films, was at various times also known as Junior Coghlan and Frank Coghlan, Jr. He appeared with James Cagney, Humphrey Bogart, Bette Davis and Mickey Rooney, and film buffs remember him for the serial "Adventures of Captain Marvel." His films with Ronald Reagan include 1938's "Brother Rat," 1939's "Angels Wash Their Faces" and 1943's "This is the Army."

I knew Ronnie Reagan through the years as a fellow actor, a good performer and a very nice person. I am proud to say that I have always voted for him.

In 1951 while I was Public Information Officer at the Naval Air Station in Jacksonville, Florida, Ronnie came through town promoting his new film. I contacted him at the theater and invited him to the station for dinner. He arrived and was very charming to all he met; he and I even had a picture taken together. My wife and I had dinner with him at the Officers Club that night with the CO and XO of the station and their wives. They were all very impressed with how genuine he was.

Soon after he became President, I wrote an old Navy friend who was then assistant to White House Chief of Staff Ed Meese and asked if he would get the photo of Ronnie and me autographed by the President. He said no problem. It was returned to me in about ten days with the following inscription: "To Frank—With very best wishes. Ronald Reagan." It now fills the place of honor in my den.

I just recalled that I own a 16mm print of probably the funniest five minutes ever. It is from the Foreign Press Association's Golden Globe Awards dinner around 1960 in Hollywood. Ronnie, as MC, introduces a very chesty, statuesque Jayne Mansfield who is to present the year's top comedian award to Cantinflas. He is not present, so little Mickey Rooney steps up to accept for him and turns to Jayne, his face coming only up to her bosom. Needless to say, Mick milks the moment.

President Ronald Reagan, left, with former Presidents of the United States Gerald Ford, Jimmy Carter and Richard Nixon. Occasion marked the first time four Presidents had been alive at the same time to pose together.

Shaking his head, Ronnie comes back on and ad libs, "Andy Hardy Goes to College."

Frank Coghlan
March 18, 1982

★ ★ ★

The word for President Reagan is straightforward. He was very straightforward as an actor, too. But I come from a country (England) where an actor couldn't get elected rat catcher.

Michael Caine
"At the Movies," by Chris Chase
The New York Times, March 19, 1982

★ ★ ★

Pat Buttram is a popular homespun toastmaster, comedian and sidekick of Gene Autry in many Western films.

I wrote one-liners for him (President Reagan). He used them in all his speeches. One was:
Recession is when you lose your job.
Depression is when your neighbor loses his job.
Recovery is when Jimmy Carter loses his job.

Pat Buttram
The John Davidson Show (TV)
March 25, 1982

★ ★ ★

The Social Security System may go broke. But you young people don't have anything to worry about. President Reagan is going to make you old before your time.

Johnny Carson
The Tonight Show Starring Johnny Carson (TV)
April 2, 1982

★ ★ ★

Kirk Douglas' films: "Champion," "Young Man with a Horn," "The Glass Menagerie," "Ace in the Hole," "The Bad and the Beautiful," "Detective Story," "Lust for Life," "Paths of Glory," "Spartacus," "Lonely Are the Brave," etc.

Now when I travel around speaking to students or to other groups, I'm asked one question that I never used to be asked before. It's whether I have any intention of going into

President Ronald Wilson Reagan speaks, 1982.

★ ★ ★

politics. They figure if one actor (Ronald Reagan) could do it, why couldn't I?

Kirk Douglas
Interview with William Wolf
April 6, 1982

★ ★ ★

Rory Calhoun acted with Ronald Reagan in the 1947 film "That Hagen Girl." Other films: "The Great John L," "The Red House," "I'd Climb the Highest Mountain," "Meet Me After the Show," "With a Song in My Heart," "Way of a Gaucho," "How to Marry a Millionaire" and "River of No Return."

I keep a low profile, although I did help my old friend Ronald Reagan when he ran for Governor of California. We did not renew old acquaintances during "on location" shooting in Washington (of my new TV series *Capitol*). He's a pretty busy man, as President of the most powerful capitol in the world. He's got a lot of problems. No, we haven't been chatting although I'm sure he'd love it.

Rory Calhoun
"Back Again as a Good Guy in a TV Soap"
by Helen Dorsey
The Boston Globe, April 8, 1982

★ ★ ★

The President was one of the first stars I ever worked with. Imagine acting with the man who would become the most powerful person in the world.

He was an awfully pleasant fellow. We both stayed at the Savoy in London in adjoining suites (while we were making *The Hasty Heart*). And although I was a young, pretty girl, he never made a pass at me. Of course there were splendid reasons. I was wildly in love with Gary Cooper and he (Reagan) was still in love with Jane Wyman, who had just divorced him.

Ron had a phenomenal memory and was deeply interested in politics, even when he was a film star.

Patricia Neal
"Patricia Neal Tells of Triumph Over Her Tragic Past"
by Joan Babbage
The Newark *Star-Ledger*, April 20, 1982

★ ★ ★

Lionel Stander, co-star in the television series "Hart to Hart," was featured in such films as "Mr. Deeds Goes to Town," "A Star is Born" (Janet Gaynor version), "The Ice Follies of 1939," "Guadalcanal Diary," "Specter of the Rose," "The Kid from Brooklyn," "Call Northside 777" and "They Shoot Horses, Don't They?"

They used to say actors should keep their mouths shut. Now we've got a President who was an actor and who can't keep his mouth shut.

But he's giving better performances than he ever did as an actor. Maybe he has better lines.

Lionel Stander
"Familiarity Breeds Success for 'Hart to Hart' Butler"
by Bob Wisehart
The Newark *Star-Ledger*, April 27, 1982

★ ★ ★

The President is urging prayer in schools. The first thing the kids will pray for is hot lunches.

Johnny Carson
The Tonight Show Starring Johnny Carson (TV)
May 7, 1982

★ ★ ★

Outstanding among James Mason's more than one hundred films: "The Seventh Veil," "Odd Man Out," "Pandora and the Flying Dutchman," "Five Fingers," "Julius Caesar," "A Star is Born," "North by Northwest," "Lolita," "Heaven Can Wait" and "The Verdict."

My son Morgan is giving Ronnie Reagan a helping hand at the White House (he has a job with the President's Administration). I only met Reagan once, at the time when I was just fading out from Hollywood. I bumped into him at a jewelry store and I took the liberty of introducing myself — under the guise of congratulating him on becoming Governor of California. He was very charming.

James Mason
"James Mason," by Michael Buckley
Films in Review, May, 1982

★ ★ ★

Among James Garner's films: "The Great Escape," "The Thrill of It All," "The Americanization of Emily," "36 Hours," "Grand Prix," "Support Your Local Sheriff," "Health" and "Victor Victoria."

A lot of 'em are kicking themselves for it (electing Ronald Reagan Governor of California twice and President).

James Garner
(Phil) *Donahue in Los Angeles* (TV)
May 4, 1982

★ ★ ★

Cary Grant's classic films: "The Awful Truth," "Bringing Up Baby," "Holiday," "Gunga Din," "His Girl Friday," "Penny Serenade," "The Philadelphia Story," "Arsenic and Old Lace," "I Was a Male War Bride" and "North by Northwest."

The movies are like any other business. The end result is to please the public. Actors must be bright or they couldn't make the money they do. People think acting is called: "Anybody can do it." So, why doesn't everyone go ahead and do it? As an actor and then President of the Screen Actors Guild, Ronald Reagan had a crash education. We all did.

Cary Grant
"Cindy Adams"
New York Post
May 13, 1982

★ ★ ★

On Joan Fontaine's distinguished film roll: "Gunga Din," "The Women," "Rebecca," "Suspicion," "This Above All," "The Constant Nymph," "Jane Eyre," "Frenchman's Creek," "Letter from an Unknown Woman" and "Ivanhoe."

I didn't know Ronald Reagan well, we never worked together, although I did go to a party at his house once. My sister (Olivia de Havilland), who was at Warner Brothers with Reagan, knew him far better than I.

It's been written that the Reagans never went to the chic Hollywood parties such as were given "by the David O. Selznicks and Joan Fontaine." I don't think they chose to. They were more involved with the rich industrialist group, not the artistic group. There's also a snobbism in Hollywood: the second leads don't get invited.

I am proud, however, that an actor is such a respected and intelligent man.

Joan Fontaine
June 1, 1982

★ ★ ★

Ronald Reagan had an audience with the Pope and almost dozed off a few times while the Pope was talking. But the Pope said, "That's all right. I slept through all your movies."

Johnny Carson
The Tonight Show Starring Johnny Carson (TV)
June 8, 1982

★ ★ ★

To June Allyson in the 1940s:
    Don't ask Ronnie what time it is, because he'll tell you how a watch is made.

Jane Wyman
". . .June Allyson Says She's Grown Up at Last"
by David Wallace
People, June 21, 1982

★ ★ ★

Richard Todd co-starred with Ronald Reagan in 1950's "The Hasty Heart." Among his other films: "Stage Fright," "Lightning Strikes Twice," "The Story of Robin Hood," "The Sword and the Rose," "Rob Roy, The Highland Rogue," "A Man Called Peter," "The Virgin Queen," "Saint Joan" and "The Longest Day."

When Ronald Reagan and I appeared together in *The Hasty Heart* in England. . .I was a newcomer, and he was a big international star, living at the Savoy, where he would be picked up and delivered by a studio car. I shared a mews flat off Belgrave Square with two other actors and used to drive myself to the studio. It was winter, the weather beastly. Freezing fog all the time. Ronnie was appalled that I should have to drive through such conditions and suggested picking me up on his way to the studio. Maybe he just wanted to see if I knew my lines, but I'll never forget his kindness.

Everyone knew that the Scot (whom I played). . .would run away with the accolades. Ronnie showed no resentment at all. He handed me everything and never hogged a scene.

We'd talk about the world as it was at that time. The Marshall Plan and all that. He was proud to be an American and one hundred per cent behind what his country was doing, but I recall he was slightly resentful of the handouts all of Europe was then taking from America. I had the feeling he was vaguely insular in his attitude. I don't think he knew a lot about the world then and had not been out of his country a great deal.

I had dinner at Ronnie's and Nancy's home in Los Angeles. . .I knew he was going to run for something eventually.

I hope he turns out to be a fine President. He has the decency and professionalism to do the job. . .I think Ronnie has brought back a sense of pride to his country.

Richard Todd
"Actor Reagan Recalled by 1948 Co-Star"
by Hugh Mulligan
Asbury Park Press, June 29, 1982

★ ★ ★

June Allyson's films: "Best Foot Forward," "Two Girls and a Sailor," "Good News," "The Three Musketeers," "Words and Music," "Little Women," "The Stratton Story," "The Reformer and the Redhead," "The Glenn Miller Story," "Executive Suite," etc.

Arguing politics drew them together. . .It was a riot to listen to Ronnie, a staunch Democrat, trying to convert Richard (Dick Powell) while Richard argued just as hard to turn Ronnie Republican. . .I do not know whether it was Richard or Nancy and her staunchly Republican family who finally switched Ronnie. I only know that Richard, chortling with glee, took full credit for it. Richard, as usual, was haranguing Ronnie about his politics when Ronnie suddenly said, "Hold on, I've switched. You don't have to gnaw at me anymore. I'm a Republican." Richard turned to me and said, "What have I done? The son of a bitch will probably end up running for President someday — and making it."

June Allyson
June Allyson, by June Allyson with Frances Spatz Leighton
G. P. Putnam's Sons Publishers, 1982

★ ★ ★

Opera star Dorothy Kirsten appeared in the films "Mr. Music" and "The Great Caruso."

One of the most glamorous leading men with whom I have worked was our new fortieth President of the United States. . .I was engaged to appear with Ron on his great show, *General Electric Theater*. I remember that experience as an especially enjoyable one. . .His warm and congenial personality, which won him many friends, was also responsible for his success in motion pictures, television, or any kind of show business.

Dorothy Kirsten
A Time to Sing, by Dorothy Kirsten
Doubleday Publishers, 1982

★ ★ ★

Dick Powell's best-known films include "42nd Street," "Gold Diggers of 1933," "Christmas in July," "It Happened Tomorrow," "Murder, My Sweet," "The Bad and the Beautiful" and four with Ronald Reagan: 1937's "Hollywood Hotel," 1938's "The Cowboy from Brooklyn" and "Going Places" and 1939's "Naughty But Nice."

They (Jane Wyman and Ronald Reagan) would not have gotten a divorce had their careers not been going in opposite directions—hers up, his down.

Dick Powell
"June Allyson: Shocking Truth Behind Tinsel of Hollywood Life"
by June Allyson with Frances Spatz Leighton
Star, July 6, 1982

★ ★ ★

I didn't vote for him. We always called him "little Ronnie Reagan," you know, and to all of us who grew up with him, it's kind of *awesome* that he's President (big chuckle). But Reagan has an enormous advantage, because he comes through on television, and a lot of screen actors are not good on live TV. It's a very strange, personal medium. Yet I think it was wonderful that Reagan appointed a woman to the Supreme Court.

Bette Davis
"Playboy Interview"
Playboy, July, 1982

★ ★ ★

Kiel Martin is one of the stars of the television series "Hills Street Blues."

I'm frightened. And every performer out here feels the same way since that jury freed that maniac John Hinckley after he tried to kill President Reagan. I would have felt much more safe and secure if he had gotten a prison term. That would have gotten the message across to all the other crazies and weirdos out there. . .He has ruined the life of Jim Brady by putting a bullet in his brain, and has gotten away with that horrible act.

Kiel Martin
"Tough-Guy Actor Living in Fear"

by Bob Lardine
New York *Daily News*, July 6, 1982

★ ★ ★

Robert Horton acted with Ronald Reagan in the 1954 film "Prisoner of War." In the 1955 television series "Kings Row" he portrayed the character Reagan first had played in the film version. Horton also starred in the TV series "Wagon Train." Other films: "The Tanks Are Coming," "Apache War Smoke," "Pony Soldier," "The Story of Three Loves," "Bright Road," "Arena."

Ronald Reagan and I worked together in a film called *Prisoner of War* at MGM. He was the star and I was a young contract player on the lot, but his movie career was beginning to wind down. He was a real up-front type of guy—as he is today. I remember talking with him about the script, which was not very good, and felt I could ask him why a star of his calibre would be doing such a mediocre story.

He replied, "I know it's a dog, but I'm not in a position *not* to do it."

A while later, during the years when I was starring in *Wagon Train* on television, his dressing room for *General Electric Theater* was adjacent to mine at Universal Studios. We talked often. He was so warm, so pleasant and always so political. And I was always so *a*-political. When he'd bring up politics, I'd say, "Ronnie, that's not my bag."

A number of years passed. Then, in the early 1970s, when he was Governor of California at Sacramento and I was starring there at the Music Center in *Man of La Mancha*, I received a very nice letter from him. He said he was happy to see that I had done the things I'd wanted with my life and complimented me on my work. He was sorry he couldn't get over to see me because he and Nancy had to leave for Europe.

The bottom line is: I can't imagine having more respect for the man—for what he is and for what he has done with *his* life.

Robert Horton
July 7, 1982

★ ★ ★

Outstanding among Bob Cummings' films are "The Devil and Miss Jones," "Moon over Miami," "It Started with Eve," "Saboteur," "Princess O'Rourke," "You Came Along," "The Lost Moment," "Dial M for Murder," "The Carpetbaggers" and, with Ronald Reagan, 1942's "Kings Row."

Kings Row and Ronnie Reagan—what wonderful memories.

It was shot in about seven weeks, incredible for a film of this scope, for only around $760,000. But with all the talent and ingenuity involved, it looked like millions.

This company was one of the most efficiently run operations I've ever been associated with. One of the main reasons was William Cameron Menzies, the great production designer, who made lovely, detailed charcoal drawings of every scene before shooting began. He had all the characters in them, and you'd look and recognize yourself—there was Ronnie Reagan, there was Annie Sheridan, there was Bob Cummings.

They cleared a big sound stage and put Menzies' drawings up on the wall—two or three hundred of them. We all sat around on chairs—the actors as well as director Sam Wood, cameraman James Wong Howe, the make-up and costume people—while Menzies showed us what we'd be wearing in various scenes. Unlike some productions then, where you were told to go out and buy whatever you needed, and to hell with the cost and time, we were told to get what we could that would be appropriate to each scene from Warner Brothers' wardrobe department.

Menzies said, "We don't need all the living room furniture," so all we'd have in a scene was a door, a piece of a drape, a chair. They built only what Menzies felt was absolutely necessary. There were lots of close-ups of the actors. It had the effect of looking arty rather than cheap. Very little was shot outdoors. Even some of the buggy-riding scenes were shot indoors at Warners, so they could control the light and the actors wouldn't have to squint during their big moments. No one tells his most intimate thoughts while his eyes are squinting and watering.

I always wanted one of Menzies' charcoal drawings, and told him so. I kept running into him and asking. Finally, I said, "Bill, where's that *Kings Row* drawing?" And he said, "I'm so sorry. I promise I'll get you one." But then he died and I never got it.

Everything went smoothly. My only problem was the make-up. The associate producer, David Lewis, a very nice, sensitive man, had a photo of his friend, the noted director James Whale, when he was a child, and he was beautiful. With his curls, he looked just like a girl. Lewis not only wanted my hair curled like Whale's as a child but also wanted to prettify me with heavy make-up. I said, "I don't want to be so made up. I'll be standing next to Ronnie Reagan a good deal of the time, and he isn't wearing *any*." But Lewis won. When the picture came out, a New York critic wrote, "Bob Cummings plays Parris Mitchell like the third girl on the left. . ." Much later, I met the S.O.B. and asked him why he wrote that. He said, "The make-up." But I think once you get absorbed in the story, you forget about it.

Ann Sheridan, our leading lady, was an adorable girl. A few years earlier, when we were both just starting out, we were under contract to the same studio, Paramount, but I never dated her. During World War II when I was in the service, I came into town one day and called her for a date. She said, "Why, Bob, I'd *love* to go out with you. Why didn't you ever ask me before?" I said I guessed we both had been too busy. Well, I was sueing Universal Pictures at the time and I was suddenly called to court the next day and had to cancel our date. We never did get to go out. Now she's gone.

Around this time the American Medical Association was trying to enjoin *Kings Row*, just released, from being shown because they alleged that it showed doctors in a bad light. Claude Rains played a doctor who killed his daughter and then himself, while Charles Coburn amputated Ronnie Reagan's legs because he didn't want him to go with his daughter. I don't think anything came of the AMA's efforts. Certainly the film was widely seen.

Ronnie and I became the best of friends. He is one of the most honorable men I've ever met. I'd trust him with my car, my house, my wife, my *life*. He writes me letters and signs them "Ron." He was great to work with. We played extremely well together which I think showed on the screen in our many intimate scenes together. We were the first of the big "buddy" movies.

I knew his first wife, Jane Wyman, too. We acted together in the film *Princess O'Rourke*; she could be a lot of fun. I never heard him say one bad word about her, but I've personally heard her say plenty against him. I don't know why she did that. I remember she told me, ". . .all he talks about morning, noon and night is world affairs."

He *did* expound on the set a lot, even in 1941. He was a passionate Democrat then and our director, Sam Wood, and I were Republicans (though I didn't work at it much). Once, Sam, Ronnie, Annie, Charles Coburn (also a Republican) and I were sitting around the set waiting for the cameraman to light the next scene. There was always a lot of good-natured political banter going on between Sam and Ronnie, especially.

This one time I said, "Ronnie, have you ever considered becoming President some day?"
He replied, "President of what?"
I told him President of the United States.
His retort: "What's the matter, Bob, don't you like my acting, either?"
Some years later my phone rang in the middle of the night. I was sound asleep; I had to film in the morning. Groggily, I picked up the receiver and someone said, "It's Ronnie."
"Ronnie who?"
He said, "Ronnie *Reagan*. I'm trying to help a senator get elected and we're giving a party for him tomorrow night. Can you come?"
I said, "You know I'm not political, Ronnie."
And he answered, "Couldn't you just come and be there anyway?"
I asked who the senator was.
"His name is Richard Nixon."
"But isn't he a Republican?"
"I've switched," said Ronnie. "I sat down and made a list of the people I know, and the most admired people I know are Republicans."

Bob Cummings
July 12, 1982

★ ★ ★

Shirley MacLaine has appeared in "Around the World in 80 Days," "The Sheepman," "Some Came Running," "Ask Any Girl," "The Apartment," "Can-Can," "Irma La Douce," "Sweet Charity" and "The Turning Point."

If only Reagan did to Nancy what he's doing to the country.

Shirley MacLaine
The Riviera Hotel, Las Vegas, 1982

★ ★ ★

Comedian Rip Taylor has worked nightclubs, television, Broadway and had a cameo role in the film "Things Are Tough All Over."

People say Ronald Reagan is old. He's not old. He was in the war and wounded twice: at Gettysburg and Little Big Horn.

Rip Taylor
Good Morning New York (TV)
July 26, 1982

★ ★ ★

I've known Reagan for about forty, forty-two, forty-three years. He was there (Hollywood) when I went out in 1937. I had him on my radio show and did a lot of things. I helped him. He called me a couple of days before he went to Cincinnati, the last couple of days of his campaign, and I went to Cincinnati. . .I don't know what he did to switch but that's shocking, to think that he once was a liberal Democrat. That's like Lawrence Welk playing punk rock.

Would I be surprised if he ran again? You know how actors like reruns.

Bob Hope
"The Freewheeling Bob Hope"
New York Post
July 30, 1982

★ ★ ★

Television's Susan Sullivan has appeared in the series "Rich Man, Poor Man, Book 2,"
"Julie Farr, M.D.," "It's a Living" and, co-starring with Jane Wyman, "Falcon Crest."

Jane (Wyman) never mentions Reagan, and nobody ever brings it up. Come to think of it, she would have made a great First Lady. She's a smart woman.

Susan Sullivan
"Acting with Glamorous Stars is Fun," by Kay Gardella
New York *Daily News*, August 5, 1982

★ ★ ★

Pearl Bailey has performed in most branches of show business. Her films include "Variety
Girl," "Carmen Jones," "That Certain Feeling," "St. Louis Blues," "Porgy and Bess" and
"All the Fine Young Cannibals."

I was so upset I sent him (President Reagan) a two-page telegram when they mentioned they were going to send the Marines to Lebanon. If one or two Marines had been killed, Americans would have been up in arms. If (only) they'd sent a ship with food and clothing. . .It also hit me in the pit of the stomach when they talked about cutting off the food of the poor people. . .We got to get our *own* people out of the trash cans. I can't come on here and tell you (the host) how to dress when I look like a mess.

Pearl Bailey
Good Morning New York (TV)
September 13, 1982

★ ★ ★

Richard Widmark's films: "Kiss of Death," "Road House," "Down to the Sea in Ships,"
"Panic in the Streets," "Saint Joan," "The Alamo," "Judgment at Nuremberg,"
"Madigan," "Murder on the Orient Express," etc.

We (Ronald Reagan and I) never worked together, but I've known him for a long time. He's a nice, affable guy, but I disagree with every one of his policies. Did I vote for Reagan? Of course not. I said I've known him for a long time.

Richard Widmark
People
September 13, 1982

★ ★ ★

Paul Newman has starred in many films, notably "Somebody Up There Likes Me," "Cat on a Hot Tin Roof," "Exodus," "The Hustler," "Sweet Bird of Youth," "Hud," "Cool Hand Luke," "Butch Cassidy and the Sundance Kid," "The Sting" and "The Verdict."

I guess I've had more fun doing this (going into business with Newman's Own salad dressing) than anything else I've done in a long time. But remember, it's really my way of telling Ronald Reagan that his salad days are over.

Paul Newman
"Newman's Salad Dressing: Oil, Vinegar and Ballyhoo"
by Mimi Sheraton
The New York Times, September 15, 1982

★ ★ ★

Among the films of Walter Pidgeon, who has appeared in the vicinity of one hundred: "Man Hunt," "How Green Was My Valley," "Blossoms in the Dust," "Mrs. Miniver," "Madame Curie," "Mrs. Parkington," "Week-end at the Waldorf," "Holiday in Mexico," "Command Decision" and "Advise and Consent."

I write him (Ronald Reagan) a note now and then because he's so terribly busy. I always knew he had the ability, and I think he's done very well so far. It's very hard because he got there at the wrong time. You know, in the old days he wouldn't fly. No, sir. He always took the train, which was so much longer. But then he went to work for General Electric and had to fly in order to get around. Imagine, if he didn't change his mind about flying he wouldn't be where he is.

Walter Pidgeon
"People: At 85, Pidgeon Calls It Quits"
by Phil Roura and Tom Poster
New York *Daily News*, October 17, 1982

★ ★ ★

Eddie Albert has been prominent in "Rendezvous with Annie," "Smash-Up, The Story of a Woman," "Roman Holiday," "Oklahoma!", "I'll Cry Tomorrow," "Attack!", "The Heartbreak Kid" and, with Ronald Reagan, 1938's "Brother Rat" and 1940's "Brother Rat and a Baby" and "An Angel from Texas."

I did several pictures with him (Ronald Reagan) and we became good friends. In fact, we were neighbors for a while. But I don't see him every morning now. The President appointed my wife Margo to a commission to serve on the National Endowment for the Arts and Sciences. At one meeting he came clear across the room and hugged her. She told him, "You-know-who sends his love," and he said: "Well, you tell you-know-who I love him back." Was I surprised at what happened to my old pal? Well, from this point on nothing will ever surprise me.

Eddie Albert
"Eddie Albert: Hanging in There"
by Martin Burden
New York Post, October 18, 1982

★ ★ ★

Hey, I just got off the line with The Gipper. That was real nice of Ronnie, calling me from the White House to wish me a happy eighty-third birthday. Especially with the astronauts in space and Brezhnev dying. It had to be a busy day. He said he's discovered that the Reagans and O'Briens are related. And I told him, let's form a Reagan–O'Brien ticket.

Pat O'Brien
"People: Gipper Calls 'Coach' Pat on 83d Birthday"
by Phil Roura and Tom Poster
New York *Daily News*, November 12, 1982

★ ★ ★

Frank Sinatra's best-known films: "Anchors Aweigh," "On the Town," "From Here to Eternity," "Guys and Dolls," "High Society," "Pal Joey," "The Joker is Wild," "Some Came Running," "A Hole in the Head" and "The Manchurian Candidate."

When Frank Sinatra wired his regrets at being unable to attend the Friars Club roast of comedian Dick Shawn, he explained:
President Reagan doesn't like me and (Secretary of State) George Shultz to be absent from the White House at the same time.

Frank Sinatra
People
November 15, 1982

★ ★ ★

Do you remember the term square? He (Reagan) was a perfect square. Just like this (she makes the square sign). Of course, I love squares. They're thoughtful, considerate, ladies-first types of guys. He was that way. And he was fun to work with. He's the same today. Success hasn't changed him at all.

Rhonda Fleming
Legends of the Screen (TV) with Nancy Collins, 1982

★ ★ ★

Myrna Loy's more than half a century in films has included six Thin Man pictures plus "Love Me Tonight," "Manhattan Melodrama," "The Great Ziegfeld," "Test Pilot," "The Rains Came," "The Best Years of Our Lives," "Mr. Blandings Builds His Dream House," "Cheaper by the Dozen."

No, I never worked with Ronald Reagan. I did a G.E. TV thing or something and he came on the set one day. No, I'm not happy (that he's President). I was willing to give him a chance. But he's destroying everything now I've lived my life for.

Myrna Loy
Legends of the Screen (TV) with Nancy Collins, 1982

★ ★ ★

I happen to like Ronald Reagan—Mr. President—very, very much. I've seen him throughout the years at parties and I adore Nancy. But I never dated him.

Lana Turner
"A Talk with Lana Turner," by Mary Ellin Barrett
Family Weekly, December 5, 1982

★ ★ ★

Joan Leslie, Ronald Reagan's leading lady in "This Is the Army" (1943), also appeared in "High Sierra," "Sergeant York," "Yankee Doodle Dandy," "The Hard Way," "The Sky's the Limit," "Thank Your Lucky Stars," "Rhapsody in Blue" and "Repeat Performance."

This is the Army was a funny kind of picture. My scenes with Ronald Reagan were quite far apart in the continuity and rather brief. Off-screen, we were acquaintances more than friends. He was an extremely competent, prepared, dignified type of actor with no particular dramatic flair in his acting, just a nice, steady approach.

Ron and I enjoyed talking together. We had the same kind of opinions about our studio, Warner Brothers.

It was known as "the factory," you know. People who were under contract were expected to do what they were told. We had little to say about the films we were put into or loaned out for. If you wanted to go higher, you had to gather your forces—your talents, your agents, whatever—to take stands. Look at Ron's first wife, Jane Wyman. She was under contract to Warners for years, and not much was happening. She was determined, though, to move out of the light parts she was getting. Her agents had to work very hard for her to get big dramatic pictures like *Johnny Belinda*. I remember her asking the make-up people to help her change her image. She started to sing again in *Night and Day*, the Cole Porter biography. You had to take the initiative. Eventually, I sued Warners to be free of my contract and be able to choose my roles. For a while, there was a kind of "gentleman's agreement" in Hollywood not to hire me, but I finally broke that with a picture for the Eagle–Lion Studios called *Repeat Performance*.

But back to Ron. We shot quite a bit of *This Is the Army* at Camp Pendleton in San Diego, California. I remember we did these intimate scenes in the hot gravel in the glaring sun. But Ron never complained. He seemed to have more knowledge of the overall problems of production than the average actor, and wasn't only concerned with his own motivation and part. As for conversations that we had, one thing I recall is that he admired Betty Hutton, who was a hot new star then at Paramount. He observed that it was very unusual for such an energetic comedienne to be so attractive as well.

Right after his last term as Governor of California, I saw Ron at a Los Angeles Museum retrospective of the films of Hal Wallis, who had been executive producer at Warners when we were there. *Yankee Doodle Dandy*, in which I played opposite James Cagney, was shown one day and I attended. Afterward, going down to the gallery for the reception, I found myself in the elevator with Ron and Nancy and some other people. He commented that he thought it would be difficult for young people of today to understand the kind of flag-waving patriotism that worked so well in *Yankee Doodle Dandy* in 1942, when we had just entered World War II. I think we do look for things to criticize today. Anyway, we said it was great to see each other again, and noted that we both still looked pretty good. It was my first meeting with Nancy, who was charming.

About a year and a half ago, a producer from Warner Communications called and said that they were putting together a film for Ron's and Nancy's anniversary and wanted me to be a part of it. It would contain clips from his Warner films into which would be cut brief interviews with six stars who knew him: James Cagney, Pat O'Brien, Virginia Mayo, Alexis Smith, Clint Eastwood and myself. Naturally I said yes. They sent me some suggested lines and we were all picked up and taken out to the studio. It was all shot in one day. Finally, they said say something like "Happy Anniversary." When it came my turn, I mentioned our discussion of patriotism in the elevator that day, and wished him all the best.

Sometime later, the phone rang at home and my daughter answered it. She called to me, "The White House is on the phone." I picked it up and Ron came on. He said it was so nice of me to do the film and how much he and Nancy appreciated it. That was all—but I chattered on and on to him about a charity I was involved in that had recently honored Nancy (everyone here in Hollywood loves Nancy). His voice sounded a bit strained—but with everyone he has to talk to, whose wouldn't?—yet he seemed relaxed. He's trying to stand up for what he believes in, and I think he's doing a very good job as President.

Joan Leslie
January 11, 1983

★ ★ ★

In 1939, Huntz Hall of the Dead End Kids and later the Bowery Boys made two films with Ronald Reagan, "Hell's Kitchen" and "Angels Wash Their Faces." Other features: "Dead End," "Angels with Dirty Faces," "They Made Me a Criminal," "The Return of Dr. X," "A Walk in the Sun" and Ken Russell's "Valentino."

We (the Dead End Kids) used to give him "hot hats." Ronnie Reagan gave us a hot foot one day. So we got a piece of paper, rolled it into a cone, put it on him and lit it.

Huntz Hall
Late Night with David Letterman (TV)
February 23, 1983

★ ★ ★

Coleen Gray, who acted with Ronald Reagan on TV and in the 1955 film "Tennessee's Partner," also was prominent in "Kiss of Death," "Nightmare Alley," "Fury at Furnace Creek," "Red River," "Riding High," "Father is a Bachelor" and "The Killing."

Ronald Reagan is a fine man and a good friend.

Coleen Zeiser (Coleen Gray)
February, 1983

★ ★ ★

Tom Selleck, who plays the title role in the TV series "Magnum P.I.," has starred in such television features as "The Sacketts," "Divorce Wars" and "The Shadow Riders," as well as the theater film "High Road to China."

I think a lot of opposition to him (Reagan) has been obstructionist. His economic policies haven't been in effect long enough to get results.

Tom Selleck
"Hello, Tom Selleck," by Sally Ogle Davis
Ladies Home Journal
January, 1983

★ ★ ★

Major Robert Mitchum movies: "The Story of G.I. Joe," "Pursued," "Out of the Past," "The Lusty Men," "Not as a Stranger," "The Night of the Hunter," "Heaven Knows, Mr. Allison," "Home from the Hill," and "The Sundowners." On TV: "The Winds of War."

I used to go to dinner on occasion with Ronnie when he was a great friend of Bob Taylor's. And it was always like we were being monitored by an eagle scout. He didn't want to tell the bad joke. You always felt a little constricted with Dutch, at least I did.

Robert Mitchum
"Robert Mitchum Gives a Rare Interview"
by Barry Rehfeld, *Esquire*
February 1983

★ ★ ★

Shirley Temple, Ronald Reagan's co-star in 1947's "That Hagen Girl," also appeared in "Little Miss Marker," "Captain January," "Heidi," "Rebecca of Sunnybrook Farm," "The Little Princess," "The Blue Bird," "Since You Went Away," "Kiss and Tell" and "The Bachelor and the Bobby-Soxer."

I saw him (Reagan) last year at the White House. He gave me a great big hug and turned me around to the group and said he was the first man to propose to me — he meant on the screen. The reaction was "Oh, no!", as if to say he was too old for me.

Shirley Temple
Entertainment Tonight (TV)
March 23, 1983

★ ★ ★

Filmography

Hollywood impresses me as being ten million dollars' worth of intricate and highly ingenious machinery functioning elaborately to put skin on baloney.

GEORGE JEAN NATHAN

1. **Love Is On The Air.** Warner Brothers, 1937. Director: Nick Grindé. Based on the story *Hi, Nellie* by Roy Chanslor. Screenplay: Morton Grant. Camera: James Van Trees. 61 minutes.

Cast: Ronald Reagan, June Tarvis, Eddie Acuff, Ben Welden, Robert Barrat, Addison Richards, Raymond Hatton, Tommy Bupp, Dickie Jones. Ronald Reagan as a crusading radio announcer.

2. **Hollywood Hotel.** Warner Brothers, 1937. Director: Busby Berkeley. Producer: Hal B. Wallis. Story: Jerry Wald, Maurice Leo. Screenplay: Wald, Leo, Richard Macaulay. Camera: Charles Rosher, George Barnes. 109 minutes.

Cast: Dick Powell, Rosemary Lane, Lola Lane, Hugh Herbert, Ted Healy, Glenda Farrell, Johnnie Davis, Frances Langford, Alan Mowbray, Mabel Todd, Allyn Joslyn, Grant Mitchell, Edgar Kennedy, Fritz Feld, Curt Bois, Louella Parsons, Ronald Reagan, Benny Goodman and His Orchestra. RR as a member of Louella Parsons' radio staff.

3. **Swing Your Lady.** Warner Brothers, 1938. Director: Ray Enright. Associate producer: Samuel Bischoff. Based on the story *Toehold on Artemus* by H. R. Marsh and the play by Kenyon Nicholson, Charles Robinson. Screenplay: Joseph Shrank, Maurice Leo. Camera: Arthur Edeson. 79 minutes.

Cast: Humphrey Bogart, Penny Singleton, Frank McHugh, Louise Fazenda, Nat Pendleton, Allen Jenkins, Leon Weaver, Frank Weaver, Loretta "Elviry" Weaver, Ronald Reagan. RR as a sports reporter.

4. **Sergeant Murphy.** Warner Brothers, 1938. Director: B. Reeves Eason. Associate producer: Bryan Foy. Story: Sy Bartlett. Screenplay: William Jacobs. Camera: Ted McCord. 57 minutes.

Cast: Ronald Reagan, Mary Maguire, Donald Crisp, Ben Hendricks, William Davidson, Max Hoffman, Jr., Emmett Vogan, Robert Paige, Janet Shaw, Rosella Towne, Edmund Cobb, Sam McDaniel. RR as a cavalry private.

5. **Accidents Will Happen.** Warner Brothers, 1938. Director: William Clemens. Associate producer: Bryan Foy. Story: George Bricker. Screenplay: Bricker, Anthony Coldeway. Camera: L. William O'Connell. 62 minutes.

Cast: Ronald Reagan, Gloria Blondell, Richard Purcell, Sheila Bromley, Addison Richards, Hugh O'Connell, Janet Shaw, Elliott Sullivan, Anderson Lawlor, Spec O'Donnell, Don Barclay. RR as an insurance adjustor.

6. **The Cowboy From Brooklyn.** Warner Brothers, 1938. Director: Lloyd Bacon. Producer: Hal B. Wallis. Based on the play *Howdy, Stranger* by Robert Sloane, Louis Peletier, Jr. Screenplay: Earl Baldwin. Camera: Arthur Edeson. 80 minutes.

Cast: Dick Powell, Pat O'Brien, Priscilla Lane, Dick Foran, Ann Sheridan, Johnnie Davis, Ronald Reagan, Emma Dunn, Granville Bates, James Stephenson, Hobart Cavanaugh, Elizabeth Risdon, Dennie Moore, Rosella Towne, Jeffrey Lynn, Mary Field. RR as a New York agent's associate.

7. **The Amazing Dr. Clitterhouse.** Warner Brothers, 1938. Director: Anatole Litvak. Associate producer: Robert Lord. Based on the play by Barré Lyndon. Screenplay: John Wexley, John Huston. Camera: Tony Gaudio. 87 minutes.

Cast: Edward G. Robinson, Claire Trevor, Humphrey Bogart, Gale Page, Donald Crisp, Allen Jenkins, Thurston Hall, John Litel, Henry O'Neill, Maxie Rosenbloom, Curt Bois, Ward Bond. RR as a voice on the radio.

8. **Boy Meets Girl.** Warner Brothers, 1938. Director: Lloyd Bacon. Producer: George Abbott. Based on the play by Bella, Sam Spewack. Screenplay: the Spewacks. Camera: Sol Polito. 80 minutes.

Cast: James Cagney, Pat O'Brien, Marie Wilson, Ralph Bellamy, Dick Foran, Frank McHugh, Bruce Lester, Ronald Reagan, Penny Singleton, Dennie Moore, James Stephenson, Bert Hanlon, Harry Seymour, Pierre Watkin, John Ridgely, Carole Landis, Rosella Towne, Peggy Moran. RR as a radio announcer.

9. **Brother Rat.** Warner Brothers, 1938. Director: William Keighley. Producer: Hal B. Wallis. Based on the play by John Monks, Jr., Fred F. Finklehoffe. Screenplay: Richard Macaulay, Jerry Wald. Camera: Ernest Haller. 90 minutes.

Cast: Wayne Morris, Priscilla Lane, Eddie Albert, Ronald Reagan, Jane Wyman, Jane Bryan, Johnnie Davis, Henry O'Neill, Larry Williams, William Tracy, Gordon Oliver, Jessie Busley, Olin Howland, Louise Beavers, Frank Coghlan, Don DeFore. RR as a military cadet.

10. **Girls On Probation.** Warner Brothers, 1938. Director: William McGann. Associate producer: Bryan Foy. Story-screenplay: Crane Wilbur. Camera: Arthur Todd. 63 minutes.

Cast: Jane Bryan, Ronald Reagan, Sheila Bromley, Anthony Averill, Henry O'Neill, Elizabeth Risdon, Sig Rumann, Dorothy Peterson, Susan Hayward, Larry Williams, Lenita Lane, Peggy Shannon, Janet Shaw. RR as a young attorney.

11. **Going Places.** Warner Brothers, 1938. Director: Ray Enright. Associate producer: Benjamin Glazer. Based on the play *The Hottentot* by Victor Mapes, William Collier, Sr. Screenplay: Sig Herzig, Jerry Wald, Maurice Leo. Camera: Arthur Todd. 85 minutes.

Cast: Dick Powell, Anita Louise, Ronald Reagan, Allen Jenkins, Walter Catlett, Harold Huber, Larry Williams, Thurston Hall, Minna Gombell, Louis Armstrong, Maxine Sullivan, Joyce Compton, Robert Warwick, John Ridgely, Eddie Anderson, Rosella Towne. RR as a member of the Maryland horsey set.

12. **Secret Service Of The Air.** Warner Brothers, 1939. Director: Noel Smith. Associate producer: Bryan Foy. Based on the files of ex-chief of Secret Service H. William Moran. Screenplay: Raymond Schrock. Camera: Ted McCord. 60 minutes.

Cast: Ronald Reagan, John Litel, Ila Rhodes, Rosella Towne, James Stephenson, Eddie Foy, Jr., Larry Williams, John Ridgely, Anthony Averill, Bernard Nedell, Frank M. Thomas, Joe Cunningham, Morgan Conway, Raymond Bailey. RR in the first of four appearances as "Brass" Bancroft, pilot turned Secret Serviceman.

13. **Dark Victory.** Warner Brothers, 1939. Director: Edmund Goulding. Producer: Hal B. Wallis in association with David Lewis. Based on the play by George Emerson Brewer, Jr., Bertram Bloch. Screenplay: Casey Robinson. Camera: Ernest Haller. 106 minutes.

Cast: Bette Davis, George Brent, Humphrey Bogart, Ronald Reagan, Geraldine Fitzgerald, Henry Travers, Cora Witherspoon, Virginia Brissac, Dorothy Peterson, Charles Richman, Herbert Rawlinson, Leonard Mudie, Fay Helm, Lottie Williams, Ila Rhodes. RR as an imbibing young socialite.

14. **Code Of The Secret Service.** Warner Brothers, 1939. Director: Noel Smith. Associate producer: Bryan Foy. Based on the files of ex-chief of Secret Service H. William Moran. Screenplay: Lee Katz, Dean Franklin. Camera: Ted McCord. 58 minutes.

Cast: Ronald Reagan, Rosella Towne, Eddie Foy, Jr., Moroni Olsen, Edgar Edwards,

Jack Mower, John Gallaudet, Joe King, Steven Darrell, Frank Puglia, Maris Wrixon. RR as "Brass" Bancroft.

15. **Naughty But Nice.** Warner Brothers, 1939. Director: Ray Enright. Screenplay: Richard Macaulay, Jerry Wald. Camera: Arthur Todd. 90 minutes.

Cast: Dick Powell, Gale Page, Ann Sheridan, Helen Broderick, Allen Jenkins, ZaSu Pitts, Ronald Reagan, Maxie Rosenbloom, Jerry Colonna, Vera Lewis, Elizabeth Dunne, Luis Alberni, Peter Lind Hayes, Grady Sutton. RR as composer Dick Powell's friend.

16. **Hell's Kitchen.** Warner Brothers, 1939. Directors: Lewis Seiler, E. A. Dupont. Associate producers: Mark Hellinger, Bryan Foy. Story: Crane Wilbur. Screenplay: Wilbur, Fred Niblo, Jr. Camera: Charles Rosher. 81 minutes.

Cast: Billy Halop, Bobby Jordan, Leo Gorcey, Huntz Hall, Gabriel Dell, Bernard Punsley, Frankie Burke, Margaret Lindsay, Ronald Reagan, Stanley Fields, Grant Mitchell, Fred Tozere, Arthur Loft, Vera Lewis, Robert Homans. RR as a social worker.

17. **Angels Wash Their Faces.** Warner Brothers, 1939. Director: Ray Enright. Producer: Robert Fellows. Based on an idea by Jonathan Finn. Screenplay: Michael Fessier, Niven Busch, Robert Buckner. Camera: Arthur Todd. 76 minutes.

Cast: Ann Sheridan, Ronald Reagan, Billy Halop, Bonita Granville, Frankie Thomas, Bobby Jordan, Bernard Punsley, Leo Gorcey, Huntz Hall, Gabriel Dell, Henry O'Neill, Eduardo Ciannelli, Berton Churchill, Margaret Hamilton, Jackie Searle, Grady Sutton, Marjorie Main, Frank Coghlan. RR as a district attorney's son.

18. **Smashing The Money Ring.** Warner Brothers, 1939. Director: Terry Morse. Associate producer: Bryan Foy. Based on an idea by Jonathan Finn. Screenplay: Anthony Coldeway, Raymond Schrock. Camera: James Van Trees. 57 minutes.

Cast: Ronald Reagan, Margot Stevenson, Eddie Foy, Jr., Joe Downing, Charles D. Brown, Elliott Sullivan, Don Douglas, Charles Wilson, Joe King, William Davidson, Dick Rich, Max Hoffman, Jr. RR as "Brass" Bancroft.

19. **Brother Rat And A Baby.** Warner Brothers, 1940. Director: Ray Enright. Associate producer: Robert Lord. Based on characters in the play *Brother Rat* by John Monks, Jr., Fred F. Finklehoffe. Screenplay: Jerry Wald, Richard Macaulay. Camera: Charles Rosher. 87 minutes.

Cast: Priscilla Lane, Jane Bryan, Jane Wyman, Wayne Morris, Eddie Albert, Ronald Reagan, Peter B. Good, Larry Williams, Arthur Treacher, Moroni Olsen, Jessie Busley, Paul Harvey, Berton Churchill, Nana Bryant, Mayo Methot, Ed Gargan, Richard Clayton, Alan Ladd. RR repeated his character from *Brother Rat.*

20. **An Angel From Texas.** Warner Brothers, 1940. Director: Ray Enright. Associate producer: Robert Fellows. Based on the play *The Butter and Egg Man* by George S. Kaufman. Screenplay: Fred Niblo, Jr., Bertram Millhauser. Camera: Arthur Todd. 69 minutes.

Cast: Eddie Albert, Wayne Morris, Rosemary Lane, Jane Wyman, Ronald Reagan, Ruth Terry, John Litel, Hobart Cavanaugh, Ann Shoemaker, Tom Kennedy, Milburn Stone, Elliott Sullivan. RR as a Broadway producer.

21. **Murder In The Air.** Warner Brothers, 1940. Director: Lewis Seiler. Associate producer: Bryan Foy. Based on the story *Uncle Sam Awakens* by Raymond Schrock. Screenplay: Schrock. Camera: Ted McCord. 55 minutes.

Cast: Ronald Reagan, John Litel, James Stephenson, Eddie Foy, Jr., Lya Lys, Robert Warwick, Victor Zimmerman, William Gould, Kenneth Harlan, Frank Wilcox. RR in his final appearance as "Brass" Bancroft.

22. **Knute Rockne, All American.** Warner Brothers, 1940. Director: Lloyd Bacon. Associate producer: Robert Fellows. Based on the story *Spirit of Knute Rockne* by Robert Buckner and material from Mrs. Rockne and Rockne's friends and associates. Screenplay: Buckner. Camera: Tony Gaudio. 98 minutes.

Cast: Pat O'Brien, Gale Page, Ronald Reagan, Donald Crisp, Albert Basserman, John Litel, Henry O'Neill, Owen Davis, Jr., John Qualen, Dorothy Tree, John Sheffield, Kane Richmond, George Reeves, Richard Clayton. RR as Notre Dame's tragic football hero George Gipp.

23. **Tugboat Annie Sails Again.** Warner Brothers, 1940. Director: Lewis Seiler. Associate producer: Bryan Foy. Based on characters created by Norman Reilly Raine. Screenplay: Walter De Leon. Camera: Arthur Edeson. 77 minutes.

Cast: Marjorie Rambeau, Jane Wyman, Ronald Reagan, Alan Hale, Charles Halton, Clarence Kolb, Paul Hurst, Victor Kilian, Chill Wills, Harry Shannon, John Hamilton, Sidney Bracy, Jack Mower, Margaret Hayes, Neil Reagan. RR as a sailor.

24. **The Santa Fe Trail.** Warner Brothers, 1940. Director: Michael Curtiz. Associate producer: Robert Fellows. Screenplay: Robert Buckner. Camera: Sol Polito. 110 minutes.

Cast: Errol Flynn, Olivia de Havilland, Raymond Massey, Ronald Reagan, Alan Hale, Guinn Williams, Van Heflin, Henry O'Neill, William Lundigan, John Litel, Gene Reynolds, Alan Baxter, Moroni Olsen, Erville Anderson, Susan Peters, Charles D. Brown, David Bruce, William Marshall, Ward Bond, Joseph Sawyer. RR as Errol Flynn's buddy, George Armstrong Custer.

25. **The Bad Man.** MGM, 1941. Director: Richard Thorpe. Producer: J. Walter Ruben. Based on the play by Porter Emerson Browne. Screenplay: Wells Root. Camera: Clyde De Vinna. 70 minutes.

Cast: Wallace Beery, Lionel Barrymore, Laraine Day, Ronald Reagan, Henry Travers, Tom Conway, Chill Wills, Nydia Westman, Chris-Pin Martin, Charles Stevens. RR as a rancher.

26. **Million Dollar Baby.** Warner Brothers, 1941. Director: Curtis Bernhardt. Producers: Jack L. Warner, Hal B. Wallis. Story: Leonard Spigelgass. Screenplay: Casey Robinson, Richard Macaulay, Jerry Wald. Camera: Charles Rosher. 102 minutes.

Cast: Priscilla Lane, Jeffrey Lynn, Ronald Reagan, May Robson, Lee Patrick, Helen Westley, Walter Catlett, Richard Carle, George Barbier, John Qualen, John Ridgely, Fay Helm, Nan Wynn, John Sheffield. RR as a tinhorn pianist.

27. **International Squadron.** Warner Brothers, 1941. Director: Lothar Mendes. Associate producer: Edmund Grainger. Based on the play *Ceiling Zero* by Frank Wead. Screenplay: Barry Trivers, Kenneth Gamet. Camera: James Van Trees. 87 minutes.

Cast: Ronald Reagan, James Stephenson, Olympe Bradna, William Lundigan, Joan Perry, Julie Bishop, Tod Andrews, Cliff Edwards, John Ridgely, Selmer Jackson, Addison Richards, Holmes Herbert, Eddie Conrad, Reginald Denny, Richard Travis, William Hopper, Frank Faylen, Helmut Dantine. RR as an American stunt pilot.

28. **Nine Lives Are Not Enough.** Warner Brothers, 1941. Director: A. Edward Suther-

land. Associate producer: William Jacobs. Based on the novel by Jerome Odlum. Screenplay: Fred Niblo, Jr. Camera: Ted McCord. 63 minutes.

Cast: Ronald Reagan, Joan Perry, James Gleason, Peter Whitney, Faye Emerson, Howard da Silva, Edward Brophy, Charles Drake, Vera Lewis, Ben Welden, John Ridgely. RR as a brash young reporter.

29. **Kings Row.** Warner Brothers, 1942. Director: Sam Wood. Executive producer: Hal B. Wallis. Based on the novel by Henry Bellamann. Screenplay: Casey Robinson. Camera: James Wong Howe. 130 minutes.

Cast: Ann Sheridan, Robert Cummings, Ronald Reagan, Betty Field, Charles Coburn, Claude Rains, Judith Anderson, Nancy Coleman, Kaaren Verne, Maria Ouspenskaya, Harry Davenport, Ernest Cossart, Ann Todd, Scotty Beckett, Douglas Croft, Mary Thomas, Joan Du Valle, Ludwig Stossell. RR as a small-town skirt-chaser.

30. **Juke Girl.** Warner Brothers, 1942. Director: Curtis Bernhardt. Executive producer: Hal B. Wallis. Based on a story by Theodore Pratt. Adaptor: Kenneth Gamet. Screenplay: A. I. Bezzerides. Camera: Bert Glennon. 90 minutes.

Cast: Ann Sheridan, Ronald Reagan, Richard Whorf, George Tobias, Gene Lockhart, Alan Hale, Betty Brewer, Howard da Silva, Willard Robertson, Faye Emerson, Willie Best, Fuzzy Knight, Spencer Charters. RR as a drifting crop picker.

31. **Desperate Journey.** Warner Brothers, 1942. Director: Raoul Walsh. Producer: Hal B. Wallis. Based on the story *Forced Landing* by Arthur Horman. Screenplay: Horman. Camera: Bert Glennon. 107 minutes.

Cast: Errol Flynn, Ronald Reagan, Nancy Coleman, Raymond Massey, Alan Hale, Arthur Kennedy, Ronald Sinclair, Albert Basserman, Sig Rumann, Patrick O'Moore, Felix Basch, Ilka Gruning, Elsa Basserman. RR as a Yank in the RAF.

32. **This Is The Army.** Warner Brothers, 1943. Director: Michael Curtiz. Producers: Jack L. Warner, Hal B. Wallis. Based on the stage productions *Yip, Yip, Yaphank* and *This is the Army* by Irving Berlin. Screenplay: Casey Robinson, Claude Binyon. Camera: Bert Glennon, Sol Polito. 121 minutes.

Cast: George Murphy, Joan Leslie, Ronald Reagan, George Tobias, Alan Hale, Charles Butterworth, Rosemary DeCamp, Dolores Costello, Una Merkel, Stanley Ridges, Ruth Donnelly, Dorothy Peterson, Kate Smith, Frances Langford, Gertrude Niesen, Joe Louis, Victor Moore, Irving Berlin. RR as the author of an army show.

33. **Stallion Road.** Warner Brothers, 1947. Director: James V. Kern. Producer: Alex Gottlieb. Based on the novel by Stephen Longstreet. Screenplay: Longstreet. Camera: Arthur Edeson. 97 minutes.

Cast: Ronald Reagan, Alexis Smith, Zachary Scott, Peggy Knudsen, Patti Brady, Harry Davenport, Angela Greene, Frank Puglia, Ralph Byrd, Lloyd Corrigan, Mary Gordon. RR as a veterinarian.

34. **That Hagen Girl.** Warner Brothers, 1947. Director: Peter Godfrey. Producer: Alex Gottlieb. Based on the novel by Edith Roberts. Screenplay: Charles Hoffman. Camera: Karl Freund. 83 minutes.

Cast: Ronald Reagan, Shirley Temple, Rory Calhoun, Lois Maxwell, Dorothy Peterson, Charles Kemper, Conrad Janis, Penny Edwards, Jean Porter, Nella Walker, Harry

Davenport, Winifred Harris, Moroni Olsen, Frank Conroy, Kathryn Card, Douglas Kennedy, Barbara Brown, Milton Parsons. RR as a war hero-lawyer.

35. **The Voice Of The Turtle.** (TV title: **One for the Book**). Warner Brothers, 1947. Director: Irving Rapper. Producer: Charles Hoffman. Based on the play by John van Druten. Screenplay: van Druten. Additional dialogue: Hoffman. Camera: Sol Polito. 103 minutes.
  Cast: Ronald Reagan, Eleanor Parker, Eve Arden, Wayne Morris, Kent Smith, John Emery, Erskine Sanford, John Holland, Nino Pepitone, Helen Wallace, Sarah Edwards, William Gould, Frank Wilcox, Ross Ford. RR as an army sergeant on leave.

36. **John Loves Mary.** Warner Brothers, 1949. Director: David Butler. Producer: Jerry Wald. Based on the play by Norman Krasna. Screenplay: Phoebe, Henry Ephron. Camera: Peverell Marley. 96 minutes.
  Cast: Ronald Reagan, Jack Carson, Patricia Neal, Wayne Morris, Edward Arnold, Virginia Field, Katherine Alexander, Paul Harvey, Ernest Cossart, Irving Bacon, George B. Hickman, Larry Rio, Nino Pepitone. RR as a soldier returning from overseas.

37. **Night Unto Night.** Warner Brothers, 1949. Director: Don Siegel. Producer: Owen Crump. Based on the novel by Philip Wylie. Screenplay: Kathryn Scola. Camera: Peverell Marley. 84 minutes.
  Cast: Ronald Reagan, Viveca Lindfors, Broderick Crawford, Rosemary DeCamp, Osa Massen, Art Baker, Craig Stevens, Erskine Sanford, Johnny McGovern, Ann Burr, Lillian Yarbo, Ross Ford, Irving Bacon, Almira Sessions. RR as an epileptic biochemist.

38. **The Girl From Jones Beach.** Warner Brothers, 1949. Director: Peter Godfrey. Producer: Alex Gottlieb. Story: Allen Boretz. Screenplay: I.A.L. Diamond. Camera: Carl Guthrie. 78 minutes.
  Cast: Virginia Mayo, Ronald Reagan, Eddie Bracken, Dona Drake, Henry Travers, Lois Wilson, Florence Bates, Jerome Cowan, Helen Westcott, Paul Harvey, Lloyd Corrigan, Myrna Dell, William Forrest, Gary Gray, Mary Stuart, Jeff Richards, Dale Robertson, Lola Albright, Betty Underwood, Joi Lansing. RR as a commercial artist.

39. **It's A Great Feeling.** Warner Brothers, 1949. Director: David Butler. Producer: Alex Gottlieb. Story: I.A.L. Diamond. Screenplay: Jack Rose, Melville Shavelson. Camera: Wilfrid M. Cline. 85 minutes.
  Cast: Dennis Morgan, Doris Day, Jack Carson, Bill Goodwin, Irving Bacon; guest stars David Butler, Gary Cooper, Joan Crawford, Michael Curtiz, Errol Flynn, Sydney Greenstreet, Danny Kaye, Patricia Neal, Eleanor Parker, Maureen Reagan, Ronald Reagan, Edward G. Robinson, King Vidor, Raoul Walsh, Jane Wyman. RR as himself in a barbershop bit.

40. **The Hasty Heart.** Warner Brothers, 1950. Director: Vincent Sherman. Producers: Howard Lindsay, Russell Crouse. Based on the play by John Patrick. Screenplay: Ranald MacDougall. Camera: Wilkie Cooper. 99 mintues.
  Cast: Ronald Reagan, Patricia Neal, Richard Todd, Anthony Nicholis, Howard Crawford, John Sherman, Ralph Michael, Alfred Bass, Orlando Martins. RR as an American soldier in a Burmese hospital.

41. **Louisa.** Universal, 1950. Director: Alexander Hall. Producer: Robert Arthur.

Story–screenplay: Stanley Roberts. Camera: Maury Gertsman. 90 minutes.

Cast: Ronald Reagan, Charles Coburn, Ruth Hussey, Edmund Gwenn, Spring Byington, Piper Laurie, Scotty Beckett, Connie Gilchrist, Willard Waterman, Jimmy Hunt, Marjorie Crosland, Terry Frost, Martin Milner. RR as a middle-aged architect.

42. **Storm Warning.** Warner Brothers, 1951. Director: Stuart Heisler. Producer: Jerry Wald. Based on the story *Storm Center* by Daniel Fuchs, Richard Brooks. Screenplay: Fuchs, Brooks. Camera: Carl Guthrie. 93 minutes.

Cast: Ginger Rogers, Ronald Reagan, Doris Day, Steve Cochran, Hugh Sanders, Lloyd Gough, Raymond Greenleaf, Ned Glass, Walter Baldwin, Lynne Whitney, Stuart Randall, Sean McClory. RR as a district attorney.

43. **Bedtime For Bonzo.** Universal, 1951. Director: Frederick de Cordova. Producer: Michel Kraike. Story: Raphael David Blau, Ted Berkman. Screenplay: Val Burton, Lou Breslow. Camera: Carl Guthrie. 83½ minutes.

Cast: Ronald Reagan, Diana Lynn, Walter Slezak, Jesse White, Lucille Barkley, Herbert Hayes, Herbert Vigran, Leslye Banning, Midge Ware, Ginger Anderson, Bridget Carr, Harry Tyler, Ed Gargan, Billy Mauch. RR as a psychology professor.

44. **The Last Outpost.** Paramount, 1951. Director: Lewis R. Foster. Producers: William H. Pine, William C. Thomas. Screenplay: Geoffrey Homes, George Worthington Yates, Winston Miller. Camera: Loyal Griggs. 88 minutes.

Cast: Ronald Reagan, Rhonda Fleming, Bruce Bennett, Bill Williams, Peter Hanson, Noah Berry, Jr., Hugh Beaumont, John Ridgely, Lloyd Corrigan, Charles Evans, Richard Crane. RR as a confederate cavalry officer.

45. **Hong Kong.** Paramount, 1951. Director: Lewis R. Foster. Producers: William H. Pine, William C. Thomas. Story: Foster. Screenplay: Winston Miller. Camera: Lionel Lindon. 92 minutes.

Cast: Ronald Reagan, Rhonda Fleming, Nigel Bruce, Lady May Lawton, Marvin Miller, Claude Allister, Danny Chang, Mary Commerville, Lowell Gilmore. RR as a cynical soldier of fortune.

46. **The Winning Team.** Warner Brothers, 1952. Director: Lewis Seiler. Producer: Bryan Foy. Based on the story *Alex the Great* by Seeleg Lester, Merwin Gerard. Screenplay: Ted Sherdeman, Lester, Gerard. Camera: Sid Hickox. 98 minutes.

Cast: Doris Day, Ronald Reagan, Frank Lovejoy, Eve Miller, James Millican, Rusty Tamblyn, Gordon Jones, Hugh Sanders, Frank Ferguson, Walter Baldwin, Dorothy Adams, Bonnie Kay Eddy, James Dodd. RR as Grover Cleveland Alexander, troubled baseball great.

47. **She's Working Her Way Through College.** Warner Brothers, 1952. Director: H. Bruce Humberstone. Producer: William Jacobs. Based on the play *The Male Animal* by James Thurber, Elliott Nugent. Screenplay: Peter Milne. Camera: Wilfrid M. Cline. 101 minutes.

Cast: Virginia Mayo, Ronald Reagan, Gene Nelson, Don DeFore, Phyllis Thaxter, Patrice Wymore, Roland Winters, Raymond Greenleaf, Norman Bartold, Amanda Ran-dolph, Henrietta Taylor, Eve Miller, the Blackburn Twins. RR as a mild-mannered theater arts professor.

48. **Tropic Zone.** Paramount, 1953. Director: Lewis R. Foster. Producers: William H. Pine, William C. Thomas. Story: Tom Gill. Screenplay: Foster. Camera: Lionel Lindon. 94 minutes.

Cast: Ronald Reagan, Rhonda Fleming, Estelita, Noah Beery, Jr., Grant Withers, John Wengraf, Argentina Brunetti, Rico Alanez, Maurice Jara, Pilar Del Rey. RR as a plantation foreman.

49. **Law And Order.** Universal, 1953. Director: Nathan Juran. Producer: John W. Rogers. Based on the story *Saint Johnson* by W. R. Burnett. Screenplay: John, Owen Bagni, D. D. Beauchamp. Camera: Clifford Stine. 80 minutes.

Cast: Ronald Reagan, Dorothy Malone, Alex Nicol, Preston Foster, Ruth Hampton, Russell Johnson, Barry Kelley, Chubby Johnson, Dennis Weaver, Jack Kelly, Valerie Jackson. RR as a veteran sheriff.

50. **Prisoner Of War.** MGM, 1954. Director: Andrew Marton. Producer: Henry Berman. Screenplay: Allen Rivkin. Camera: Robert Planck. 80 minutes.

Cast: Ronald Reagan, Steve Forrest, Dewey Martin, Oscar Homolka, Robert Horton, Paul Stewart, Henry "Harry" Morgan, Stephen Bekassy, Leonard Strong, Darryl Hickman, Jerry Paris, Stuart Whitman, John Lupton. RR as a North Korean POW.

51. **Cattle Queen Of Montana.** RKO, 1954. Director: Allan Dwan. Producer: Benedict Bogeaus. Story: Thomas Blackburn. Screenplay: Howard Estabrook, Robert Blees. Camera: John Alton. 88 minutes.

Cast: Barbara Stanwyck, Ronald Reagan, Gene Evans, Lance Fuller, Anthony Caruso, Jack Elam, Yvette Dugay, Morris Ankrum, Chubby Johnson, Myron Healey, Rodd Redwing, Paul Birch, Byron Foulger, Burt Mustin. RR as a government undercover agent.

52. **Tennessee's Partner.** RKO, 1955. Director: Allan Dwan. Producer: Benedict Bogeaus. Based on the story by Bret Harte. Screenplay: Dwan, Milton Krims, D. D. Beauchamp, Graham Baker, Teddi Sherman. Camera: John Alton. 87 mintues.

Cast: John Payne, Rhonda Fleming, Ronald Reagan, Coleen Gray, Anthony Caruso, Leo Gordon, Myron Healey, Morris Ankrum, Chubby Johnson, Joe Devlin, John Mansfield, Angie Dickinson. RR as the stranger known as "Cowpoke."

53. **Hellcats Of The Navy.** Columbia, 1957. Director: Nathan Juran. Producer: Charles H. Schneer. Based on a book by Charles A. Lockwood, Hans Christian Adamson. Screen story: David Lang. Screenplay: Lang, Raymong Marcus. Camera: Irving Lippman. 82 minutes.

Cast: Ronald Reagan, Nancy Davis, Arthur Franz, Robert Arthur, William Leslie, William Phillips, Harry Lauter, Michael Garth, Joseph Turkel, Don Keefer, Selmer Jackson, Maurice Manson. RR as real-life Commander Casey Abbott.

54. **The Young Doctors.** United Artists, 1961. Director: Phil Karlson. Producers: Stuart Millar, Lawrence Turman. Based on the novel *The Final Diagnosis* by Arthur Hailey.

Screenplay: Joseph Hayes. Camera: Arthur J. Ornitz. 100 minutes.

Cast: Fredric March, Ben Gazzara, Dick Clark, Ina Balin, Eddie Albert, Phyllis Love, Edward Andrews, Aline MacMahon, Arthur Hill, Rosemary Murphy, Bernard Hughes, Gloria Vanderbilt, James Broderick, Joseph Bova, George Segal, Matt Crowley, Dick Button, Addison Powell, Dolph Sweet, Ella Smith, Nora Helen Spens, Bob Dahdah. RR was the unseen narrator.

55. **The Killers.** Universal, 1964. Director-producer: Don Siegel. Based on the story by Ernest Hemingway. Screenplay: Gene L. Coon. Camera: Richard L. Rawlings. 95 minutes.

Cast: Lee Marvin, John Cassavetes, Angie Dickinson, Ronald Reagan, Clu Gulager, Claude Akins, Norman Fell, Virginia Christine, Don Haggerty, Robert Phillips, Kathleen O'Malley, Ted Jacques, Irvin Mosley, Jimmy Joyce, Scott Hale, Seymour Cassel. RR as a powerful underworld figure.

56. **It's Showtime** (TV title: **The Wonderful World Of Those Cuckoo Crazy Animals**). United Artists, 1976. Producers: Fred Weintraub, Paul Heller. Writer: Alan Myerson. Editors: Alan Holzman, Peter E. Berger. 86 minutes.

Compilation film of old clips spotlighting animal stars and also showing Irene Dunne, Cary Grant, William Powell, Myrna Loy, Mickey Rooney, Elizabeth Taylor, Roddy McDowall, Betty Grable, Mae West, John Wayne, Errol Flynn, Gregory Peck, Penny Singleton, Arthur Lake, James Cagney, Joan Blondell, Ray Milland, Humphrey Bogart, Buster Crabbe, Bing Crosby, Van Johnson, Dick Powell, Gene Autry, Charlie Chaplin, Walter Slezak. RR in scenes from *Bedtime for Bonzo*.

Doug McClelland, freelance author-lecturer-consultant on film, grew up in Newark, New Jersey, where he became an arts editor of *The Newark Evening News*, and later was founding editor of *Record World* magazine in New York City. He has contributed to such periodicals as *Films in Review, After Dark, Films and Filming, Screen Facts, Film Fan Monthly, Quirk's Reviews, The World of Yesterday, Hollywood Studio Magazine* and *Filmograph*.

McClelland's first book was *The Unkindest Cuts: The Scissors and the Cinema* (A.S. Barnes, 1972), dealing with the practice of cutting scenes and sometimes actors' entire performances from motion pictures. His second, *Susan Hayward: The Divine Bitch* (Pinnacle, 1973), was the first book on the late, distinguished Hollywood star. His third book was *Down the Yellow Brick Road: The Making of The Wizard of Oz* (Pyramid, 1976), which detailed the events behind the classic 1939 film. McClelland's fourth book was *The Golden Age of "B" Movies* (Ottenheimer, 1981), which tells the story of that most neglected of film species, the low-budget but high-quality motion picture — the "B."

Anthologies in which McClelland's writings have appeared include *The Real Stars, The Real Stars #2, The Real Stars #3, The Old-Time Radio Book* and *Hollywood Kids*.

Doug McClelland has been a consultant on more than two-dozen film-related books, and has lectured at colleges, women's clubs, libraries, film symposia and film festivals.

★ ★ ★